BETTE DAVIS SPEAKS

ALSO BY BOZE HADLEIGH

Hollywood Lesbians

BETTE
DAVIS
SPEAKS

Boze Hadleigh

Published by Barricade Books Inc.
150 Fifth Avenue
New York, NY 10011

Copyright © 1996 by Boze Hadleigh

Printed in the United States of America

Library of Congress Cataloging-in-Publication Data
Hadleigh, Boze.
Bette Davis speaks / by Boze Hadleigh.
   p.   cm.
Includes index.
ISBN 1-56980-066-9 (cl)
1. Davis, Bette, 1908- —Interviews. I. Title.
   PN2287.D32A5 1996   95-49976
                                                      CIP

First Printing

To my mother, Fresia, and Flora Belle Stockwell Boze, both admirers of Bette Davis, each a woman of strength, character and beauty.

*A*s always, to Ronnie and Linda.

Special thanks to Douglas Whitney, photo collector, and to Sue Kutosh, artist.

And to Carole and Lyle Stuart.

Thanks also to: Robert Aldrich, Joan Blondell, Carlos Clarens, Manuel Cordova, Joseph Cotten, George Cukor, Olivia de Havilland, Susan Hayward, Stan Kamen, Paul Kohner, Peter Lawford, David Lewis, Howard Mason, Doug McClelland, Gary Merrill, Agnes Moorehead, Jim Pinkston, Irving Rapper, Michael Redgrave, Harold Schiff, Gale Sondergaard, Hal Wallis, Emlyn Williams and Tennesee Williams.

CONTENTS

*B*ette Davis
is a national treasure; she is
what movies are all about!
—*The Philadelphia Inquirer*

INTRODUCTION

I first spoke with Bette Davis on my twenty-first birthday. It was the most exciting present of several that year, even if it only lasted a few minutes and was via telephone. I was in Manhattan working for *Mademoiselle* and establishing contacts which would serve me well after I completed my master's degree in journalism in San Jose, California.

My uncle was a friend of Paul Kohner, the actress' ex-agent, and got me her phone number from him in 1975. I had the number a few months before using it. I wasn't the first fan to be intimidated by Davis's enormous persona and seeming ferocity. Later, she assured me, "My bark is worse than my bite, it really is," a sentiment echoed by others whom I interviewed about her. Gleefully, she admitted, "I don't mind scaring people. It comes in handy—in the business, and in life."

———————

In New York, I began freelancing for *Talk*, a magazine distributed in most every beauty salon in the country, but nowhere else. I also wrote for *Motion Picture*, the oldest movie magazine, founded in 1910 (they eventually offered me their managing editorship). I inquired whether either periodical's editor might be interested in an interview with Bette Davis. Silly question.

So I called her up and discovered she was quite accessible to her fans. Insiders have said she usually got along better with adoring fans than with relatives or co-stars—who were "the competition."

In time, books would reveal that Davis was all but impossible to live or work with. However, as an interview subject she was a delight, as I found out several times between 1975 and early 1989, the year of her death.

One of Bette's fans-turned-confidant hit the nail on the head when he said that one-on-one, Davis was a doll. It was the presence of a third party which somehow goaded her into ruthless assertion of her dominance and power. She was quick to challenge or humiliate people who worked for her or weren't chronicling her words for posterity—so many times during our sessions, she would stop me and ask, "Have you got all that down?" or "Does that make sense? Does it *sound* all right?"

Once, at her West Hollywood apartment in the historic Colonial House on Havenhurst Drive, fashion designer Patrick Kelly stopped by with some sketches for her. Kelly created some of the more intriguing and flattering hats and outfits which the skeletal superstar wore on the Carson, Letterman and other TV talk shows in the late eighties. To a surprising extent, Bette was oohing and aahing over his designs. She forcefully eyed me, indicating I must come look. I put down my materials, rose, and looked. "They are beautiful, aren't they?" she purred.

Kelly looked ecstatic, and as Davis handed the approved sketches back to him she announced, "A queer may not know how to undress a woman, but you do know how to *dress* one, don't you, Patrick?"

The designer, who later died of AIDS, smiled wanly, then exited. Within seconds, Bette was again engrossed in our interview. I must have been momentarily dazed, for she snapped, "You *are* taking notes, aren't you?"

Months later, I read that Kelly, whose clientele included Davis, Madonna, Jane Seymour and Grace Jones, was asked to name his favorite client. His answer: Princess Diana.

A cousin of mine was once a close friend of Orry-Kelly, who created most of Bette Davis's Warners wardrobe in the 1930s and '40s. When early on I told her of the connection, she warmed to me and said, "I don't live in the past. But I love ties to the past, and someday you *must* tell me everything your cousin told you about the great Orry-Kelly. He helped make me a star, you know." We never got around to it, though I brought up the designer's name a few times—each of which led Bette down memory lane and into her career.

Many years later, after reading Charles Higham's Cary Grant biography, I noted to Bette my surprise that Orry-Kelly had lived with Grant in New York. She patted my arm. "You didn't know they were lovers?" She shook her head maternally. "My dear, *all* those New York gays know each other."

In the early eighties, editor Robert Hayes of *Andy Warhol's Interview* assigned me to interview Davis. Unaware of my multiple sessions with her, he warned, "I know people who are friends of hers. Or were, before she banished them. Try and keep it professional—don't get too close. Because once you're her friend, she thinks she owns you and can say or do anything she wants to you."

It was advice I'd already heard, and heeded. I'd wanted to know far more about Davis than most brief interviews and pre-assigned questions would allow, and was heartened to find that she would easily and happily chatter for hours at a time, answering most any question put to her, so long as its basic focus was Bette Davis, Legend.

One Hollywood columnist who became her frequent dinner guest informed me that Bette didn't like "to mix food and nostalgia." Her concentration was intense, and whatever she did, she strove to excel at it. She was an excellent cook and hostess, and a consummate interviewee, but not both at the same time.

Another fan-turned-intimate complained to me that at most she might set aside part of one day a week to reminisce and answer his questions about her past. That reporter had been hoping to do a book about the making of the cult classic *Whatever Happened To Baby Jane?* and was full of questions about Davis's vitriolic relationship with Joan Crawford. But once she befriended the man—and almost all her fan-friends were men—she clammed up. "I'm too valuable to her as an escort for her to use me as a writer," he bragged and lamented.

I lunched once at Bette Davis's in the late seventies. She prepared an impressive array of cold cuts and deli breads, plus a thoroughly curried rice which she knew I loved, and margaritas, my favorite alcoholic beverage. She did everything herself, vehemently refusing help, basking in my sincere compliments and forcing seconds and thirds on me. When I expressed surprise at the amount of housework she deigned to do, she chided me. "You shouldn't wonder. I'm a New England Yankee, and if I'd had my way, I would have become housekeeper of the century, instead of the greatest actress!"

She smiled broadly, and I couldn't tell if she was being serious or not.

At that particular time, when her temperament made it virtually impossible for her to hang on to hired help for long, she suddenly and desperately offered me a job as her companion-assistant. I was dumbfounded and flattered, and immediately declined. "But think of it!" Her eyes sparkled seductively behind a screen of smoke. "If we went to Europe, you and your five languages, how practical it would be for us...."

I smiled, shaking my head. Her eyebrows dropped an inch. "Well, you love to travel, you've told me so yourself. The pay would not be paltry, and the *experience*"—she rolled her eyes,—"would be wonderful. What more could you want?" She fixed her gimlet eye on me. "You're not still attached, are you?" I'd mentioned the relationship I'd begun in 1975, that I was still in it and expected to remain so (still am, twenty years later).

"Love!" she snorted affectionately, "stifles many a career." But several times that day, in 1978, she tried to argue the subject of coming to work for her. I had to decline more firmly. Her eyes popped wide and her generously rouged lips turned down at the corners in growing umbrage, until I reminded her that I lived some five hundred miles to the north, in San Mateo, and loved the area where I now had some roots.

Instantly mollified, she patted my hand and said, "You're right. Why spoil a beautiful friendship just so you can be my slave?" Then she threw back her head and cackled throatily, just as she did in *Baby Jane*.

To return her hospitality, I invited Bette to lunch at the Brown Derby on Hollywood and Vine the next time I was in town. She loved the food—lobster, a favorite of hers—and the ambience, but complained loudly about the slow, elderly waiters. "They belong in a morgue!" she snapped, more than once.

Seated in the cushy red booths of the now-defunct Derby, we reminisced about our first interview. She said that she'd been amused that *Talk* was available only in beauty parlors. "That's why I'd never seen it," she giggled. "I never go to those idiotic places." Bette didn't have to go to hairdressers, the hairdressers came to Bette. Besides which, in her private life—unlike, say, Joan Crawford—Bette didn't often bother "doing myself up." She saved the glamour for special public occasions, reasoning that "My fans love me because of my personality, not my looks or *clothes*, for heaven's sake!

"I always looked the way my character [in a film] *should* look—ugly or pretty. I certainly didn't waste time trying to be a little glamourpuss." In her autobiography, she'd boasted that she "brought more people into theaters than all the sexpots put together."

While still on the subject of *Talk* and its distribution, she stated—for my benefit and the waiters'—that she considered dyeing her hair a waste of time. Wigs, she asseverated, were "*much* more practical." Then she lowered her voice and stage-whispered, "Do you know that Marilyn Monroe used to dye her pubic hair?" She howled with glee. "My God! It's a wonder she didn't die sooner—from poisoning of the vulva!"

Whenever I wanted to ask Bette about somebody who was more or less her equal, like Marilyn or Joan or Hank or Errol, I usually had to work up to it by first asking about the relevant Bette Davis movie, then inquiring about a specific co-star. I could thus extract a pearl and later—as in this book—present it with or without the accompanying layers of build-up.

After learning how willing Bette Davis was to discuss most everyone and everything under the Hollywood sun, and how endlessly fascinating she was at it, I considered an eventual interview book. Most of our sessions together weren't for a particular assignment, and those which were, yielded three or four times as much material as I could fit into a given article.

In 1980, Citadel Press published *Conversations With Joan Crawford* by Roy Newquist. I bought, read and enjoyed it, then gave my copy to Bette, who grudgingly agreed to "go over it" after I noted some of its contents (not mentioning the less flattering of Crawford's quotes about her arch-rival). She kept the book for two weeks, but declined to make it part of her library. When we next talked on the phone, she herself brought up the topic:

"It is interesting, for a book about *her.*"

"Did you read it all?"

She paused before admitting that she had, stressing that it was the only book on the subject that she had ever read or had any intention of reading. (On TV she later denied having read *Mommie Dearest*, though I was told she'd done so in bed, too engrossed to light up more than one cigarette.)

Without any ulterior motive, I declared that a book titled *Conversations with Bette Davis* would probably be even more interesting. Perhaps she took exception to the word "probably," for she bellowed, "You're damn right it would!"

I later asked if she'd been at all serious about us doing an interview book. Her eyes lit up briefly, then she shrugged. "If you insist…, but do you have the time?" I explained I was currently working on a book for the same publisher about Jane Fonda. Bette quickly changed the subject.

During a subsequent conversation she mused, "Of course, nobody would have published that Crawford book while she was *alive*." She stared searchingly at me as if wondering whether there would be enough interest to publish a Davis interview book during her lifetime.

I said that, unfortunately, too many great stars are ignored until their passing. Bette said nothing. Then, "Of course, *if* you published such a book while I'm still here, I'd want at least half the profits." She glared. I smiled. She backed down a bit, winked, and said, "I guess I'm too demanding at times."

I suppressed the urge to ask, "At times?" Although she was nearly always polite to me, by then I'd heard horror stories about her reactions to those who dared confront her. I wondered silently when the first *Bette Dearest* book would appear. Not till her death, I imagined, proven wrong by publication of her daughter's first of two books.

In 1987, Bette Davis and I both had books out, and West Hollywood's largest bookstore prominently displayed them in their window. For over a month, their two hardcover best-sellers were Bette's *This 'N That* and my *Conversations With My Elders*, an interview collection with six famous men of cinema—a designer, two actors and three directors. I sent Bette a note saying I was honored to be in her company and glad for the success of her book. Days later, she called and told me she'd read some reviews of my book (not saying whether she had or would be reading the book). "My God!" she exclaimed. "You certainly tell *all* about those men, don't you? *My* book is much more discreet, Mr. Hadleigh."

It was the first time in years she'd used my last name, and just as I'd been about to broach the possibility of a *Conversations with Bette Davis*. Her indignation and her sharp pronunciation of "Hadddleigh" discouraged me, and I put the idea on a back burner. Rather than antagonizing and losing her—for she did not mellow with age, as anyone who knew her will attest—I bided my time until the next interview.

I didn't wish to proceed with a book about her that didn't have her blessing. Besides which, she'd forbidden me to use some of her juicier quotes during her lifetime, e.g., she once described Joan Crawford as "Hollywood's first case of syphilis." Our last session, in 1989, was polite, informative and occasionally ribald, but the subject was holding something back, in her manner. Somehow I had transgressed. Perhaps because my first *Conversations* book wasn't about her?

Much as I wanted to, I didn't bring up the topic of a book. I believed, despite the outer frailty which encased her iron will, that there would be another session ere long. And if not in 1989, then in 1990. I could easily picture Bette Davis living into her late eighties, as had Mae West, or even her nineties, like Lillian Gish or Beatrice Lillie. Bette had conquered one shattering affliction after another, had kept working and battling.

Then suddenly, in late 1989, while in Europe receiving yet another award, she died, from a cancer almost no one knew she'd had. Hers and Mae West's were the only deaths I ever found hard to believe. Those two celluloid artifacts had seemed next to immortal. It wasn't right or possible that Bette Davis was really gone, that there would be no more films or TV appearances, no more conversations in person and over the phone. Or that she had died at "just" eighty-one. That her body had finally overpowered the most indomitable will and personality that Hollywood ever produced.

Dear Bette Davis. I knew you better than most, not as well as some. I chose not to enter your intimate circle, but rather, to get to know you just well enough so that someday I could share your intimate and honest feelings and opinions about your life and career with the fans and admirers who now more than ever wonder: Whatever was Bette Davis really like, and what did she think about it all?

Bette Davis once told me matter-of-factly, "I am the queen of Hollywood." Welcome, then, to her kingdom....

February 14, 1996
Beverly Hills

PRIVATE LIVES

Q: You had one sibling, a younger sister, Barbara.

A: We called her Bobby.

Q: Somewhere I read that most movie stars behave like or wish they were an only child. Was this at all true of you, Miss Davis?

A: [*shifting in chair, then lighting a cigarette*] Occasionally. Because, you see, every eldest child *is* an only child—for a time. Then along comes the newer child, whom you sometimes view as an intruder.

Q: When your sister came along, did you resent her at all?

A: No, not really. She was a novelty to me. And even smaller than me. Do *you* have a younger brother or sister?

Q: A younger sister.

A: Then you know that however much we may love the

younger one, it's also that we love to dominate a younger
sister.

Q: I'll bet you did, too!

A: [*half-smiles*] I had a dominant personality. This is not
unusual in an elder or eldest child. Bobby was definitely
more the go-along type.

Q: It seems that among two people it's never a question of
total equality, don't you think?

A: Absolutely. There is no such thing as fifty-fifty. Not with
siblings, and not in any marriage *I* have known about!

Q: We can talk a bit about your marriages later, can't we?

A: I suppose we'll *have* to, if we're on the topic of my private
life!

Q: I guess we should start with your parents. I'm sure you've
discussed them before, but what was their marriage like?

A: Awful. [*pause*] They did not love each other. I've said
before that I never saw them once express any affection for
each other. It's true. After I first said that, somebody who
should know better accused me of saying it to garner sympathy. Hah! I have nevah wanted or needed sympathy from
anyone. I was just telling the awful truth.

   Some actors lie about their parents and make up a
cheery story because they think it reflects better on them.
That is nonsense. My parents' marriage in no way reflected
on me. How could it?

Q: What was your father's name?

A: Harlow. His full name was Harlow Morrell Davis. He had
no fondness for children. None. I came along in the first
year of their marriage, and he was *not* delighted. I've heard
he said I should be put up for adoption.

Q: That must have hurt....

A: Not really. He didn't know me yet. An infant is not an individual. And in a sense, he was just being practical. He felt
it—*I*—would interfere with his being a law student. I
myself did not have a family until I was very firmly established in my career. Thank goodness! Otherwise, I might
not have gotten to do or achieve what I did. Children *do*
interfere with a career—at least, they do for a mother.

Q: By the way, how much older than Bobby were you?

A: Year and a half. You?

Q: Three and a half years.

A: Oh, that is a big difference.

Q: Added to which is the fact that the elder is a male, so it
probably made it tough for my sister. I mean in terms of
being rather dominated.

A: [*shakes head, smiling*] I cannot agree with you. I think a little girl can be more easily and lastingly dominated by her
older sister than her older brother.

Q: Because they're the same gender?

A: Because between the sexes there is always a struggle. It's a
symbolic thing. Whether it's brother and sister, or husband
and wife, they struggle and they never get *that* close,
because of the differences that divide them.

Q: So in your opinion, the war between the sexes doesn't
always have to do with sex?

A: That's right. It has to do with being different, and when
there's a difference, you view it as a contest.

Q: That's a very competitive viewpoint.

A: So is life.

Q: Barbara was nicknamed Bobby, and you were—

A: Ruth Elizabeth Davis, nicknamed Betty and born April 5th, long ago! My mother got the different spelling of Betty from *Cousin Bette*, which was by Balzac. Hell of a name, isn't it?

Q: Bette?

A: Balzac! [*grins defiantly*]

Q: It does hang in one's memory....But how come, if your father was against having a first child, you were so soon followed by a sister?

A: [*shrugs*] These things happen. They *did*—especially before birth control. Also, I think most parents would think it unnatural to have one child, then not give it a companion.

Q: Were you grateful for Bobby?

A: ...Eventually. And you?

Q: Very grateful for Linda. Do you think only children suffer a lot?

A: No idea. I'm sure it's entirely dependent on the individual circumstances.

Q: I've heard it helps develop the imagination, though.

A: Perhaps. But I had a very lively imagination!

Q: Your parents divorced?

A: When I was ten.

Q: Was it a trauma?

A: No. I did miss my father, to some degree. But not his strictness. I was much closer to my mother, and if I had to have one parent, I would have chosen her, every time, and I think that is true for most every child.

Q: Could you tell me about your mother? I remember when you got the American Film Institute's Life Achievement Award, she was the one to whom you gave ultimate thanks.

A: Well, Ruthie was above all the one I have to thank. I think a father's influence can be negligible, but if you have an encouraging mother, that is a *great* help. A great help. On the other hand, if one has a discouraging mother, that must be simply dreadful.

Q: Without your mother, would there have been no Bette Davis, actress and legend?

A: [*smiles widely*] No, I have to be honest. I would have become an actress, and I would probably have succeeded.

Q: One hears of fierce mothers who push their girls into stardom, then the girls rebel and either virtually disown their mothers—like Judy Garland—or they back off from the limelight once they've made it big and pleased the mother—like Sandra Dee.

A: Oh, I was not unwilling! My mother and I worked in tandem. We *both* wanted me to be a star, and I never rejected her or what we achieved. *No!* She helped me so much. It wouldn't have been as…well, I don't want to use the word "easy." It was not easy! But without my mother, Ruthie Favor Davis, it would have been harder. And it would have been less enjoyable. Definitely.

Q: You must miss her.

A: Every single day.

Q: It reminds me of the quote, "Success means nothing without someone to share it with."

A: [*nods gently*] My mother was very…full of life. She was intelligent, she had energy. She was *good* at things.

Q: Like what?

A: She was a fine public speaker. Which certainly was not true of most women then. But my mother had great self-confidence, and I'm sure she passed it along to me. Although oddly enough, my sister had much less of it.…Anyway, she was a wonderful public speaker, she painted, she was a very good photographer, and she was simply my hero.

Q: Did she instill in you a desire to act?

A: …I became addicted to the theater when I saw Ibsen's *The Wild Duck* . It starred Blanche Yurka, who was extremely famous. Later on, she was famous for having killed someone and gotten away with it.

Q: Can you elaborate on that?

A: Not really. I only heard rumors. Nothing to go on record about.…But at any rate, I decided then and there that I would be an actress. My mother encouraged me in anything I chose to do, within reason, but it took time for her to realize that I really meant this as my life's work.

Q: What was your debut?

A: I was a fairy in *A Midsummer Night's Dream*. A dancing fairy! [*laughs*] I became addicted to applause.

Q: How did your mother support you and your sister after your father left?

A: Oh, she was very resourceful! We would never have starved. She became a governess in New York City. But she had several jobs, and we had to move several—no, countless—times because of the new jobs. Of course, as soon as

I could earn, I took over certain financial burdens, and then I supported my mother and sister, from then on.

Q: Did having been abandoned by your father ever make you feel unwanted, or even bitter?

A: Neither. No. It did give me an impression—later to be confirmed more than once—that men are not the most responsible among human beings....

Q: I know that you were briefly employed by director George Cukor [*pre-Hollywood*], but what was your connection with Eva Le Gallienne?

A: [*dourly*] There really was none. I applied to her dramatic school. She wasn't *that* much older than me, though she acted it [*ELG was born in 1899*]. But I did a cold-reading for her, and she was uncomplimentary. The worst thing she said, which *wounded* me at the time, was that I was lacking in sincerity. About the theatre! Can you imagine?

Q: Did she later apologize, as Cukor did for firing you?

A: [*shakes head*] No. She was entirely wrapped up in her little world....Is she still alive?

Q: Some say it's a matter of opinion, but yes.

A: Hmm. Then the truth will have to wait until *after*... [*arches a knowing eyebrow*]

Q: You mean about her private life?

A: Even in the twenties, she made headlines. But don't ask me, if she's still alive. [*The headlines referred to a Sapphic relationship, detailed in the book* We Can Always Call Them Bulgarians.] But let me tell you something interesting about Bobby. She once saved my life. [*dramatic pause*]

Q: How and when?

A: And why? I had a car. An Auburn, a roadster. It burned up, and Bobby somehow had enough savvy to drag me to safety in the very nick of time.

Q: You must have been enormously grateful.

A: Of course [*matter-of-factly*].

Q: You made your film debut in 1931. Did you buy a house in Hollywood or rent an apartment?

A: I rented a home, once I could afford it, and of course Ruthie and Bobby lived with me.

Q: You got married quite soon after hitting Hollywood, didn't you? Were you longing for, uh, male companionship?

A: It was in 1932. But I was twenty-four, and that was *not* rushing into marriage. Not by New England standards!

Q: What did he [*Harmon "Ham" Nelson*] do?

A: He was a musician. Trumpet. Then he formed his own band. But I'm afraid he was not very successful. Not by the standards that *I* was starting to achieve.

Q: Sort of a *Star Is Born* story, where the wife rises faster than the husband?

A: Not quite. *That* story is about a husband who was a star, then the *wife* becomes a star. Poor Ham was never a star. Though he had enough success to satisfy most men.

Q: You've reiterated that no husband could compete with Bette Davis. Obviously, in 1932, you weren't yet a big star, but during your subsequent marriages, did you think that each husband could overcome having such a famous wife?

A: You see, I kept hoping…fooling myself, more like it. It always followed a pattern. Ham was a *good* musician. But others with equal or slightly more talent became much,

much better known. And *I* became better known, and then famous, and in public he would try and belittle me.

Q: Women put up with far more than men do, don't they?

A: Women are raised to feel guilt *far* too easily! We are taught that to be "shameless" is the worst thing, but it isn't until one loses one's shame that one is really free.

Q: From others' opinions and judgments?

A: Exactly.

Q: So when he belittled you, that ended that?

A: No, the marriage didn't end right away. I kept hoping he'd improve, because women expect so much of men. We don't come face-to-face with reality till middle-age or so—even though it's been staring at us right along!

Q: You've said that if you hadn't been reared a Yankee prude, you probably wouldn't have married....

A: [*smiles*] No. I would have lived with them. Which is the *smart* thing to do. But I was smart only about my career. The rest of my life was often a shambles! And really, in all fairness to Ham, after we married, I moved him into a big house which was also home to my mother and sister. So really, he had his fill—of the impossible Davis women!

Q: What if he'd said, "Me or your mom and sister?"

A: I'd have shown him the door.

Q: Who was Number Two?

A: It sounds like a serial! [*laughs heartily*] Oh, dear. Well, he was an innkeeper. Arthur Farnsworth. We did *not* divorce. I've only divorced *three* times. He died. And I really don't want to talk about that. He died in an accident, and it was very sad and disturbing. [*Among other Davis biographers,*

Charles Higham has noted that Davis had an affair with Howard Hughes during her second marriage, and that Farnsworth, who did work for the CIA, died under mysterious circumstances.]

Q: Were there ever any actors you met or worked with that you might like to have married?

A: I did marry an actor—my last husband.

Q: I know. I mean actors whom you didn't marry but maybe wanted to?

A: [*suspiciously*] You mean that I was…attracted to? [*suddenly laughs*] Oh, yes! I wondered about a *lot* of men. What sort of husband material they might make. I didn't want to marry an actor, because I thought they were impossibly vain. On the other hand, they could understand the strains and demands of acting, the motivation.

Q: Plus, if an actor was a superstar, he wouldn't have to feel competitive with you, as you obviously wouldn't be up for the same roles, am I right?

A: [*smiles wanly*] Yes. But the big stars were either taken, or they were queer. Ty Power was both, and I heard he was a nice husband. But then, he never married any actress who could rival him in any way, including beauty. He only married those little foreign starlets.

Q: With or without his bisexuality, would you have considered marrying Power?

A: Well, he wasn't my co-star, so I didn't really know him. He was at Fox, and I, of course, was Warners [*smiles*]. I don't know—I can be plenty jealous enough of another woman, if there *is* another woman. Heaven help her! But how I'd react to another man... [*laughs*] probably not too well! But Power was much too pretty for me, even if he'd been heterosexual.

Q: Do you think it's true that most women want a husband whose looks don't detract too much from their own?

A: *I* did! My God. What I did not need was some beautiful creature of a husband to make me feel even less attractive. No, thank you very much!

Q: Yet, you were very attractive.

A: We know that *now* ....

Q: Gary Merrill was quite handsome, you know.

A: Oh, *very* handsome. Before he lost that to alcohol. But he wasn't beautiful. There is a difference.

Q: You married actor Gary Merrill, but were there any other actors you ever thought of wedding?

A: ...Henry Fonda. He was painfully shy. *And* beautiful, at that time! But he needed a passive little thing at his side. I'm afraid I must have terrified him.

Q: Any other actors?

A: [*sighs*] The only one that comes to mind was Franchot Tone. We worked together too, and I liked him very much as an actor and a man.

Q: He was...Joan Crawford's second husband, wasn't he?

A: [*frowns*] They did marry.

Q: Like you, she had four husbands, and one of them died.

A: Mmm. Well, if we had that in common, that's probably *all* we had in common.

Q: Other than being huge stars. Legends.

A: ...Thank you. I think. [*puffs at cigarette*]

Q: I can see why your marriages would have been hard on a husband without a strong ego. But Crawford's first was Doug Fairbanks, Jr., who, when they married, was a bigger star than her. And Franchot Tone was, like her, a star....

A: He was a *real* actor.

Q: Unlike her, you mean?

A: [*dismissive gesture with cigarette*]

Q: So I wonder why her marriages to those two star actors didn't work out?

A: [*a pause, then an elaborately indifferent shrug*] I can only assume that she wasn't a much better wife than a mother.

Q: Four husbands and four children...

A: [*grinning devilishly*] Yes. By the numbers. She did everything by the numbers—even acting. And she liked everything symmetrical. Poor old Joan.

Q: She *was* older than you, wasn't she?

A: Of *course* she was! She lied about her age all the time, but she was at *least* four years older than me. [*Crawford was born in 1904, Davis in 1908.*]

Q: That number four again...

A: Well, if you're interested in *my* marriages, the third one [*William Grant Sherry*] was the father of my daughter [*B.D., for Barbara Davis, the infamous author of* My Mother's Keeper].

Q: What did he do?

A: Not much—he was an artist....My mother thought he would be bad for me, and me—stubborn as a mule—I just had to prove her wrong. She kept on criticizing him, and so I married him. She was *right*!

Q: Was he physically abusive?

A: Almost from the start.

Q: There seems to have been more of that, then.

A: I don't know if there was really more, but the terrible thing was, it was all but acceptable. There weren't even laws against it.

Q: Why did you stay with him?

A: Our daughter.

Q: He was younger than you?

A: [*stoically*] Seven years. Like the fourth one. [*smiles*] As I got older, they got a *bit* younger.

Q: You helped pioneer the older woman/younger man concept, didn't you?

A: I wasn't aware of it, if I did. But men my age were too stuffy. And bossy.

Q: I recently re-read your autobiography *The Lonely Life*. In it, you said something like, "Sherry elected himself king of the household."

A: I said that he crowned himself king, and that I often wanted to crown him, myself!

Q: I'll bet. When did you marry him?

A: ...1945. The World's War ended, and ours began.

Q: When did you wed Gary Merrill?

A: Five years later, in Mexico. It was just a few weeks after the divorce from Number Three came through. [*smiles*] But Number Three was really Number *Two*, if you take my meaning....

Q: Your fourth and final marriage was your longest, right?

A: Yes, about ten years. And it really was my best, generally speaking. Perhaps I should have tried an actor sooner. Gary was very sure of himself.

Q: Yet you had some well-publicized, colorful fights.

A: Put two people together who are sure of themselves, and both dominant, and it's bound to happen. Sometimes it was fun. We always enjoyed being together because we were so often apart. And besides, arguing leads to lovely reconciliations.

Q: Arguing is dramatic.

A: Well, I love the dramatic.

Q: The two of you adopted a son [*Michael*] and a daughter [*Margot, who was mentally retarded*].

A: [*nods*]

Q: You remained friends with Merrill, didn't you?

A: [*sighs*] *Years* after we divorced—*after* the bloody custody fights—we did observe a friendly truce. [*Merrill defended Davis against* My Mother's Keeper *and urged the star's fans to boycott the "scurrilous" book* .]

Q: I understand your sister didn't have much better luck with her marriages....

A: No. None of us really did. [*laughs*] Call it the Davis Curse. No—please don't call it that. It was said in jest.

Q: If it was tough being the wife of a superstar, how much more difficult to be her sister, and live one's whole life long in her shadow?

A: Yes. But what could I do about it?

Q: Did you two get along in later years? I heard there was an estrangement.

A: Not that, no. But it's true. We weren't as close. It's sad. But we never grew *too* far apart.

Q: She did have a nervous breakdown, didn't she?

A: Yes [*almost warningly*].

Q: What about your mother? I mean, did your relationship go smoothly, all along?

A: That's just it, isn't it? *Relationships!* [*shakes head wearily*] They are *not* smooth, they take *work.* You have to mend the rough patches, then travel on. You love someone—and you never lose a mother, the way you can lose a husband or a sister—but you have hard times too.

Q: However, if the love is strong enough, the relationship prevails.

A: Yes, a bit worn out, but it does prevail. Still, the easiest thing, by far, is to live alone!

Q: Which do you think is more difficult: a woman's relationship with her mother and sister, or with her offspring?

A: What a question! You really do have a fiendish curiosity! [*laughs*] Oh, let me see…it's certainly harder to control your children than your parent or husband, but…they're *all* difficult relationships. That's just the way life is.

Q: You would not describe yourself as an easygoing person, would you?

A: I doubt it. [*smirks*]

Q: Would you say you're a loner?

A: Yes, but by necessity, not out of choice. I knew very long ago, even before I titled my book *The Lonely Life,* that I would wind up alone.

Q: You have friends....

A: Friends are wonderful. But they are very part-time. And I would not want a friend who was *that* close to me, who was on top of me. I could only live with a man, and he would have to be my husband or my lover—and I'm certainly not thinking of anything in the physical department! Not for *years*, now.

Q: Do you have female friends?

A: Does it surprise you?

Q: It doesn't much, it's just that—

A: I am not one of those women who has to be the lone queen bee of her hive, my dear.

Q: Besides which, there have been few if any actresses of your stature.

A: Yes, but...there's a wonderful line in [All About] *Eve*. Somebody tells Margo to stop treating her guests like her supporting cast. I *nevah* do *that*.

Q: Most of your friends are men, though?

A: There's one thing that's useful about a man friend—he can serve as an escort. He doesn't have to be heterosexual, it has nothing to do with romance, just practicality. In fact, the best friendships, *I* think, are 100 percent platonic.

Q: Do you have many gay friends—actors, say?

A: [*nods with a smile*] They are very good friends. And [*pause*] they love my movies!

Q: I'll bet that's a requirement for being your friend!

A: [*chilly, a bit hurt*] Not really. I do like valid criticism. Some of my movies were better than others. We do not sit around watching them. Not most of the time [*smiling again*].

Q: I didn't mean that your friends are just fans.

A: Well, some fans do want to become friends. But if they are *only* fans, then it gets old very fast. I'm bound to disappoint them, in person, and they end up boring me. Sometimes it's good to keep a distance. Most fans want their idols to be just that; they look down on human beings.

Q: When you go out now, is it usually social or professional?

A: I can't complain, or shouldn't, but it's typically for professional purposes. The older I get, the more awards I'm given for enduring—or something—and I usually take a friend to accept my award with me. That is, he accompanies me.

Q: How do you meet such men, of whom I'm sure there's no shortage?

A: It's easy, because men of all descriptions are always wanting to meet me. Or they write to me.

Q: It must be gratifying, getting so many awards?

A: …Yes. Of course it is. But it's getting to where my home looks like a big trophy room. And there is *one* thing I prefer getting to another award.…

Q: What's that?

A: [*half-sadly*] A good role.

Q: That's what Mr. Cukor told me. He said they were putting him on such a lofty pedestal that younger movie-makers hardly viewed him as part of the real world anymore.

A: That is a very real danger. They see you as a film clip, as film *history*, not as part of the working world. It's the drawback of being a legend. They admire you to death—sometimes literally—but they think you're no longer in the running. Which I very much *am*!

Q: When the song "Bette Davis Eyes" became a hit—the biggest hit of its year—it further confirmed your status as a film and a pop-culture legend.

A: That was another case of too much. It was fine, at first. Then I had to tell people that I was more than a song. There were children who never heard of me, except from the song!

Q: Hard to believe, because you've kept working, so consistently, and plenty on TV.

A: Mmm [*a slight downturning of the lips, beyond the usual, at mention of "TV"*]. I can only hope that anyone who is young and interested will see my films.

Q: Your work is the real you, right?

A: Absolutely. Those films. Add them up, and you have my entire life. Nothing is hidden. Every mood and emotion, every relationship,…it's all there.

Q: *Baby Jane* too?

A: *All* of them!

Q: Add up your ex-husbands, and what do you have? If I may venture to ask?

A: You may. You ask some outrageous questions, but you're not disrespectful. Well, if you add up those marriages, you have…What was it Shakespeare said? "Better to have loved and lost." I always held on to my hopes. Until I was fifty or so. Once a woman is past fifty, she'd better become realistic. Gary was my last fling at matrimony, and then I had to swear off. Any woman who marries after fifty is just deluding herself.

Q: Did romance end at fifty for you?

A: God, you're nosy! No. It did not. Anything else you want to know?

Q: After fifty, why didn't you just live with a man?

A: Find me the right man, and I will!

Q: Are they so hard to find?

A: I once sang a song about it: "They're Either Too Old or Too Young." What the song didn't say is that most of them are also gigolos.

Q: You mean the men in the life of a woman of, as the French say, a certain age?

A: An *un*certain age, is more like it! If a woman's over fifty and a man is sniffing around her, she had better question his motives, fast! If a woman that age is rich, she can be pretty certain what his motives are....

Q: On the other hand, Miss Davis, if you can afford him, why not indulge? Men do.

A: [*laughs*] Sometimes I wanted to. But...I'm just me. I am the product of my upbringing, for better or worse. Just a New England Yankee.

Q: You've said that every woman ought to get married. But some who've tried it, like Mae West or Katharine Hepburn, far prefer solitude.

A: Or living with another woman, as with one of the women you mentioned [*Hepburn*].

Q: Ahem, yes. Do you think a heterosexual "spinster" can ever be truly happy? Or is it a sexist question?

A: Not to me, it isn't. Personally, I can't imagine anything worse than lifelong virginity. Except death! And *that* at least we all share, so it's not so lonely.

Q: If you had to do it over again—

A: Allow me to interrupt you, Boze. Do you know what I hate? I hate when on television they ask an actress, "If you could do it all over again, what would you change?" and the silly twit says, "Nothing. I wouldn't change a thing." Who do they think they are fooling?

Q: I agree. A life of no regrets can't be much of a life. But if you had it to do over again, would you have become…a mother? Surprised you, didn't I?
[*both laugh*]

A: Yes! I thought you were still asking about the men in my life. A *mother*? I'll tell you this: I honestly do not believe that most actresses should become mothers. We don't have enough time to give, and I'm sure—no matter what they say—that an actress' child resents this.

Q: What about working women who aren't actresses?

A: That's quite different. An actress, if she is successful, is consumed by her career. She isn't just working to pay the bills. It's far more than that. It's a creative vision, a great big ambition, it's her reputation, the fight for good roles, the struggle against age and mediocrity and indifferent producers. My career was not only my job.

Q: However, you give the impression of having tried to be a good mother and wife. Without wishing to put down Ms. Crawford, but she did give the impression—to name just one star—of using her husbands and children as props for publicity and image. Or am I unfair to her, as I didn't know the lady at all?

A: [*pause*] No, you're not being unfair. Perhaps Joan *did* try. But she was *no* mother. Not at all. Not in a maternal sense. And as God is my witness, I *did* try to be the best mother I could. I did try to be a good wife. I put up with an awful lot—but so did my husbands....We don't go through life doing our very best at every moment. That's impossible! But God knows, I gave it the old college try.

Q: You succeeded at your career as few others have. Does that help compensate for a personal life that wasn't quite as successful or perfect?

A: [*smiling*] You're damn right it does.

HER HUSBAND: GARY MERRILL

*E*arly 1989. A telephone conversation with Gary Merrill, Bette Davis's fourth and last husband. Seven years her junior, he dies within five months of her, in March 1990. At the time of our talk, he has joined the list of authors of books about Davis with his *Bette, Rita [Hayworth], and the Rest of My Life*.

The memoir details his ten-year marriage to Bette and their lives in the aptly named Witch Way House on Maine's Cape Elizabeth. Merrill's portrait of the star is not flattering, but eschews the lurid approach of her daughter B. D. Hyman's book about Bette. The gallant Merrill was the first to admit his book "wouldn't become a best-seller" because "I don't paint Bette as a monster."

BH: You even went so far as to picket bookstores stocking *My Mother's Keeper*.

GM: I felt strongly that I had to do my share, and I told people eager to read it to please not buy a copy, to check it out at the library instead.

BH: You still care for her....

GM: Bette's a damn difficult woman, at times a nuisance, and not a role model of stability. But she tried to be a good mother, and spoiled her daughter rotten.

BH: Was she a good wife?

GM: She was as good a wife as she knew how to be.

BH: Were there good times?

GM: There were lots of good times. The old gal has a great sense of humor. I wouldn't have married her otherwise.

BH: Why did the marriage end?

GM: You'll have to read the book! There's lots of reasons, and they're in the book.

BH: Do you think, for compatibility, she should have married an actor sooner?

GM: I dunno. She's the one who keeps saying she should never have gotten married. She also says marriage is the only way to live. Crazy girl.

BH: At times, she contradicts herself.

GM: She's not aware of it. Bette's problem, or one of them, is she always speaks her mind. She thinks the public will love her for it.

BH: Don't they?

GM: Usually. But there's a limit.

BH: Unlike many stars who seem glossy or manufactured, Bette Davis has a very down-to-earth quality.

GM: She's an earth mother. That's the image of herself she likes best. She likes to mother people, and she mothers her fans. She loves her fans.

BH: I know.

GM: You're one of 'em? You said you'd interviewed her over the years....

BH: I am. It's been a particular pleasure, full of surprises, to get to talk with her time and again.

GM: She's a first-rate interview subject. She may grumble about sitting still for an interview, but she loves to rehash her past.

BH: She makes it interesting too.

GM: What do you want to know about her or our marriage?

BH: Well, do you think the blame for the breakup was evenly divided?

GM: I'm no angel. Ask Bette! I'm confident she has a few choice names for me.

BH: She always says you were the best of her four husbands.

GM: She didn't always say that....[*laughs*] Did she tell you I was one of twins? I didn't find out myself until I was grown up. I once asked Bette what she thought happened, why my baby twin sister died. She said, "You probably killed her in the womb—your first female victim."

BH: That's rough.

GM: That's Bette.

BH: Looking back, was the marriage more positive than negative?

GM: It was a good human experience. Mostly because of our kids. I love kids. Though Bette liked to spoil them too much.

BH: Did marriage to a big star boost your career?

GM: [*laughs*] We weren't the Liz and Dick of the 1950s, but you better believe I was thrown into a maelstrom of publicity!

BH: Your first film together [All About Eve, *1950*] was a doozy, almost impossible to top.

GM: *Life* said Bette gave the best performance any American actress ever gave in a movie. Bette agreed.

BH: Your real-life affair paralleled your screen affair. Was it easy to fall in love with Miss Davis?

GM: It was for me. She's a passionate, sexy gal, and she was at a vulnerable time in her life—past forty, on her own as a freelance actress....We had a fantastic affair, then we decided to move in together.

BH: Marriage?

GM: That's right, and then the troubles began. Small at first, but they grew.

BH: Could you elaborate?

GM: Bette's a control freak. She wants to dominate. Once in a while, she'll play humble, but she's a *star*, for heaven's sake. Has been for almost sixty years, and she's no wallflower or shrinking violet.

BH: You're pretty dominant yourself.

GM: We clashed...but we had the kids, we had our marriage— not in that order, and the kids were adopted, but we loved them dearly. [*Davis had already given birth to B.D.*] Michael is my pal now, and Margot, well, I'm sure you know the story [*Margot is mentally retarded and institutionalized.*] And we both loved Maine. We both have a strong sense of our roots.

BH: The consensus seems to be that it's nearly impossible to live with Bette Davis. That she's a great lady, and fun to be around, but not full-time. Is that so?

GM: You don't hear me denying it, do you? [*laughs*] We should have had a longer affair, not lived together or wed. But the kids...I don't regret that. I do regret all the lost time and effort, and the rage on both sides over our custody fight [*over Michael*]. Bette was such a witch about it, which is putting it as politely as I know how.

BH: Was it simply a custody battle, or also a symbolic war?

GM: What it is, is Bette hates to lose. Ever. She has to have her way, and she thinks she knows best. She bossed me, her mother, her sister, everyone in her life, though least of all the kids! She's a phenomenon, with the energy and dedication she gives to her career and legend. But she puts forth almost as much energy into ruining a close relationship.

She just can't help it, and I always wish her well. But when I left Bette—or she left me, depending whose story you believe—I got back my *sanity* . That's all.

GOLDEN *D*AYS

A: Well, the so-called Golden Age of Hollywood was not necessarily that golden! [*exhales a puff of smoke meditatively,
then shakes head*] No, it was damn trying at times. We were
properties of Warner Bros. We were contractually bound.
We were indentured. Of course, I fought to help end that
feudal system, and so did Olivia [*de Havilland*]. And we
helped to improve it, but the studio system was a form of
slavery, undeniably.

Q: Tyrone Power was quoted as saying that Hollywood was a
gilded cage.

A: That's right. Yes. Only a gilded cage. How very true. As we
rose to the top of the ladder, we were paid wonderfully
well. But always there was hanging over you the threat of
suspension. If we refused to work often enough or if we

conducted ourselves scandalously or if we defied or incurred the displeasure of a so-called mogul. Although actually, "mogul" is too regal a word for most of the men who ran the studios!

Q: What about actresses who refused to sexually service those powerful men?

A: Well, more careers were nipped in the bud *that* way than any other. That's why I'm so thankful I never had to rely on my looks. I survived on talent and on temperament. If I'd had to make it on the casting couch, I'd have screamed "Rape!" and that would have ended my career! Oh, it was terribly unfair—much more unfair on the actresses....

Q: Your willingness to be confrontational must have been an asset.

A: It was. I am that way, by nature. In Hollywood, it served me well. But I'll tell you a secret which is also good advice for most any career: scream long and loud, but only scream about the really important things. Let the details go. They don't matter over the long run. It's the crucial things you should be willing to walk the plank for.

Q: In other words, don't be petty?

A: In movies, there are ten million details. I'd have been committed to the looney bin if I'd tried to get my way in all the details. People pretend I worried about everything. Nonsense! Details are for directors to worry about. That is one reason I nevah wanted to direct.

Q: Do you think you could have gotten to direct, if you'd asked or insisted?

A: Well, Ida Lupino did it.... Of course, I was more indispensable on the screen than she was, for I believe she often directed other people's films. Yes, eventually I could have directed, if I'd wanted it enough. But I'd have had to struggle for it, and do some sustained screaming. [*laughs fondly*] To be honest, I was too selfish to direct. Not in a bad way, though. I was always concerned with the overall picture, with the film itself. Not just my performance. But *my* role is what really obsessed me. And as a director, you have to take everybody into consideration, even the supporting actors, and I was too busy with my part to do that.

Q: Do you think as a director you could objectively have directed yourself?

A: No, I don't. No, not until much later in my career, and by that time, they wouldn't have let me direct. If an actress ever gets to direct, she has to be young and she has to be a box office power as a performer. And even *then*. Look at Miss Streisand and all she went through [*with* Yentl].

Q: You were never directed by the great Dorothy Arzner, who did direct Hepburn, Roz Russell, Clara Bow and other female stars. Do you regret that?

A: [*shakes head, then smiles*] No. I do not want to outrage feminists, because I *believe* in all that. But frankly, I preferred being directed by a man.

Q: Why?

A: Because I tended to get a crush on my director, and it would have been quite inconvenient for me to develop a crush on the capable Miss Arzner!

Q: Who was, by the way, lesbian.

A: Yes. She even looked like a man, or at least dressed like one. But then, so did Miss Dietrich and Miss Hepburn, so that is not an insult.

Q: Do you think your being so confrontational hurt you in your career, Miss Davis?

A: Not when I had power, at Warners. When you do have power, you can get away with it. You know, men stars are confrontational, right and left. Yet it isn't even commented on. But with a woman, a certain reputation develops. And yes, it did hurt me, in my *later* career. By the time I was past forty, I had a reputation as a sheer horror. Totally unjustified, but it caused many people to want not to work with me.

Q: It was "totally" unjustified?

A: [*laughs*] Do I *act* like a monster? No, it wasn't justified. It was…it was just part of the Bette Davis legend, if you want to put it that way. It became very fashionable to say that you had directed me and survived. But later, many of my directors admitted I was really a pussycat to work with— and nothing at *all* what they had expected!

Q: Didn't a few find you tough?

A: If they did, they were insecure or rank amateurs. I certainly could be tough when I had to be!

Q: What do you think of the Noel Coward quote that he loved criticism so long as it was unqualified praise?

A: I agree!

Q: Do you read movie reviews?

A: Do you?

Q: Me? Not really.

A: Well, I have even less of a motive to do so than you.

Q: Without wishing to get too personal—

A: Why stop now? [*grins*]

Q: When you had an extramarital affair, did you ever have to worry that the studio might find out and take disciplinary action?

A: No…and I'm not saying I had any affairs during marriage. If I did, it was and is *my* business. But the ones you had to worry about were the press. Even then, not too much. The studio protected us—its stars—because we were valuable assets. The studio kept the press in line.

Q: How?

A: Well, say a particular reporter was indiscreet. By that, I mean he tried to report a star's indiscretion. If he did, the studios, as a block, would freeze him out. He would no longer have access to us for interviews. Nor would he be invited to premieres or screenings. And he'd probably be shunned by fellow journalists, who are very competitive anyway.

Q: Wouldn't a magazine editor be apt to quash such a story before it saw print?

A: Yes. That did happen—to others. Unless it was a story too well known to hide. Like Ingrid Bergman's pregnancy [*by her director, not her husband*]. You know, Miss Bergman was almost single-handedly responsible for all the errant wives and husbands in Hollywood returning to their legal mates! She was made an example of, and that terrified everyone. If the media could do that to her—to banish her and almost terminate her career—then they could do it to equal and lesser stars too.

Then, in the 1950s, *Confidential* magazine also put the fear of God into those with something to hide.

Q: For instance?

A: Not just an affair, but homosexuality, a prison record...

Q: How about alcoholism and drugs?

A: Yes, but my God, the alcoholism in those days was nothing compared with today's drug scene!

Q: So many older stars, from Robert Young to Dick Van Dyke, have come out as former alcoholics....

A: That's what you *did* then. You drank. We all did. The pressure at work was tremendous, there were the inevitable insecurities. I had very few of those, but most everyone drank too much. I did very rarely, and it was nevah something that developed into a problem, of course. But drinking then was so common, nobody in Hollywood commented on it. It certainly never got written about. Even [*Mary*] Pickford, for heaven's sake, became a boozer!

Q: Joan Crawford was one of the foremost women drinkers, wasn't she?

A: That's what I heard, but she could hold it very well. I'm sure it didn't interfere with her work. We didn't socialize— obviously—so I nevah saw her imbibing. But *that* was not her favorite offscreen activity anyway [*smirks*].

Q: Sex?

A: [*nods*] Her only hobby, besides collecting children. Oh, and knitting. On the set of [Whatever Happened to Baby Jane], she must have knitted her way through a flock of sheep!

Q: You've been written up as a heavy drinker, but not an alcoholic.

A: Of course not! I already explained that to you. *Nicotine* is my addiction of choice.

Q: Because drugs or alcohol are more destructive?

A: They are. Because they interfere with your work, *my* work. I would *nevah* do anything which interfered with my work or my ability to do my work.

Q: If anything, smoking has enhanced your work, or at least your screen image.

A: The best example of that is the lovely final scene in *Now, Voyager* with Paul Henreid lighting the two cigarettes. One of several examples.

Q: Cigarettes also created memorable glamour. When I visualize Marlene Dietrich, I see her smoking a cigarette, inhaling, with her cheekbones beautifully highlighted.

A: Oh, how I envied her smoking technique! She did it so languorously. I did it quicker, more nervously. But then, I envied her so much! I could almost have had a crush on her.

Q: She was one who attracted both men and women.

A: [*no reaction*]

Q: I think that the way you smoked was suited to drama, while Dietrich did it in a way suitable to movie stills.

A: That is very perceptive. Yes. I did not stop to consider how I looked doing something while acting. Whereas I imagine she always did.

Q: Did you ever take pleasure in appearing beautiful?

A: [*taken aback*] What?

Q: When you looked really beautiful, did you—

A: You think I was so beautiful? When?

Q: In *Jezebel* you were stunning. That unforgettable scene in the lacy white dress, when you sink to the floor in front of Henry Fonda and the dress puddles around you...your expression was very moving, and your face was simply beautiful.

A: [*touched*] Thank you. I'm glad that somewhere along the way I've impressed my fans as being beautiful.

Q: You were, often. In *Now, Voyager*, after your transformation, in *Marked Woman*, as a blonde in the early films, and even in *Of Human Bondage*, and as Leslie Crosbie in *The Letter*, etc.

A: You really think so?

Q: I'm not just saying it. I mean, it wasn't usually classical or obvious beauty—by that I mean not a cheap or manufactured beauty, like Jean Harlow, who personally I've never thought beautiful. But you were in fact beautiful.

A: [*nods slowly, as if weighing the opinion*] I *was* beautiful, but not a beauty. There's a difference there. But it is very pleasant to hear. And you know what, Boze? I have to agree with you! Today, I do think I was beautiful. *Then* I didn't, and I always wanted to look like someone else.

Q: Do you think if you'd liked your looks, you'd have played Elizabeth the First or women older than yourself?

A: That's the entire point about my appearance. Because I was dissatisfied, I was ready to experiment as an actress. I was very ready to look awful. Or plain or older. I sometimes did my best to look my worst! Sometimes I even outdid myself, and it hurt. Naturally, it was worse when I was older. When I first saw myself as Baby Jane, I *cried*.

Q: I don't blame you.

A: Thanks!

Q: No, it's a tribute to your integrity as an artist that you'd ever present yourself that hideously before a camera. Most star actresses wouldn't have.

A: You know why? They cared so desperately what the public thought. I didn't. I cared more what my peers thought—not of me as a person, as a performer. As an artist.

Q: Good for you! What you said about doing your best to look your worst reminds me of a line used to advertise one of your movies—"No One's as Good as Bette When She's Bad!!"

A: [*laughs*] I love that! They came up with wonderful lines. "The Actress You Love to Hate," and so on.

Q: Did you ever get hate mail when you played villains?

A: Oh, yes. Tons. But it's not important now. People are more sophisticated today, audiences know you aren't what you play on the screen.

Q: Yet some stars play the same role over and over, and one wonders if it isn't really them.

A: It can be. But images are always deceiving, to some degree.

Q: That's right—I read that John Wayne longed to play Noel Coward.

A: I'm sure Mr. Coward would have won.

Q: *Touché*! So what it boils down to is that real artistry requires a flexible ego about one's looks?

A: Yes. Did Marilyn Monroe ever look anything less than beautiful in a movie? I think not.

Q: If she had, maybe she might have grown as an actress?

A: Yes, and if she'd lived to middle age, she would have had no choice. After forty, an actress sometimes *has* to look plain or play a dull, homely housewife type. Which is depressing. But professionally, it's a good thing.

Q: This does happen with many actresses, doesn't it? Like Jane Fonda and Sophia Loren, even Raquel Welch—beautiful women who after forty take on non-sexy roles and finally develop their talent. Otherwise, like Bardot, they must retire.

A: True, but Jane was a major talent long before forty, and she changed her image long before that.

Q: Fonda was born while you were filming *Jezebel*. Have you ever wanted to work with her?

A: Yes. She's very good. I suppose I could have played her mother. *On Golden Pond*, for instance. I know [*Barbara*] Stanwyck wanted to, very much. But it hasn't happened yet, and it probably will not, I fear.

Q: Weren't you at one point a bit upset with Ms. Fonda?

A: [*puzzled momentarily*]Oh, *that*. Yes, well…It was going around that she wanted to remake [*All About*] *Eve* and play Margo Channing. I have nothing but admiration for Jane, but I could not *believe* she would wish to undertake something so ill-advised. *Eve* is perfect as it is. And apart from *Applause*, which was a musical stage version of *Eve*—and about which I had misgivings—I feel *Eve* should be left alone. At least, and certainly, during my lifetime. If only out of courtesy.

Q: As good an actress as Fonda is, I can't see her as Margo.

A: Of course not. *I* am Margo.

Q: What about Ted Turner possibly colorizing *All About Eve*?

A: If he does, I will break his legs. [*pause, then laughs, but not easily*]

Q: Can we return to your Warners heyday? Tell me about Hedda [*Hopper*] and Louella [*Parsons*].

A: Bitches…Do you mean how did I get along with them?

Q: Yes. Were you ever on the outs with either of them?

A: Everyone was on Hedda and Louella's shit-list at some point. Except Marion Davies, and that was because she was [*William Randolph*] Hearst's mistress, and Hearst was Louella's boss and Mr. [*Louis B.*] Mayer's friend. So nobody crossed him.

Q: It's a wonder that Orson Welles got away with making *Citizen Kane*, isn't it?

A: But he made it, and it was brilliant. You'll notice, though, he didn't make any more major pictures after that, or get topflight roles in major films….

Q: How did Hedda and Louella amass so much power, which now seems inconceivable?

A: It's a very long story. In essence, what the public thought in those days was very, very important. What *ignorant* people thought, I should say. There wasn't television, people weren't as informed. They were certainly not as liberal about sex or moral matters. So, what either of those women wrote took on a great importance, because like today's preachers on television, they lived as they wished but convinced people that they were guarding their morality. People are always looking for a leader or an authority, and those ladies were not shy. They were very visible, unlike the studio heads, who were men who hated the limelight or had foreign accents which they didn't want heard by the public.

Q: It's ironic that the moguls were nearly all Jewish then, but they pushed assimilation on the screen, to the point that anyone too different had to make themselves over or remain on the stage.

A: Are you at all anti-Semitic?

Q: God, no—I'm half-Jewish. But I am against those who deny the diversity of humanity, and in those days the moguls never allowed Jews to be portrayed on the screen. They had no pride in themselves, they were always running scared.

A: It is quite true that Hollywood did not take any minority to its collective bosom, unlike today.

Q: And even today, some groups function in the same brainwashed manner—like the secretly gay film executives who are the first to decline a gay-themed script.

A: But you must admit that when it comes to the whole gay question, today it is far, far better.

Q: More visible anyway. Gay characters are at least allowed to exist—in a twilight zone. But about Hedda and Lolly, did *anyone* in Hollywood like them?

A: Only as regards a career and building it up. The men [*at the studios*] loathed them, called them bitches and worse. They considered them a necessary evil.

Q: It was said that if an actress favored Hedda with a revelation about her private life, she risked offending Louella, and if she told Louella first, she made an enemy of Hopper. How did you cope with such a situation?

A: I was lucky in being a very big star. They couldn't hurt me much. Not if I didn't give them ammunition.

Q: Did you cooperate much with the publicity machine?

A: Not once I didn't have to, after my pictures sold themselves. Even the ones that weren't huge hits always made a profit.

Q: But in your early days, you did quite a bit of cheesecake.

A: Everyone did, except Garbo and Kate Hepburn. They refused to display their bodies....We were posed like beauty queens, and this to me was a completely new experience and not unflattering. I found out it was what new actresses did, and I went along with it, for I was very ambitious. ·

Q: Did it ever embarrass you?

A: Not as a woman. I had a good figure!

Q: You had a bigger bust than most people remember.

A: Kind of you to notice [*grins*]. No, I didn't mind all that idiotic cheesecake, but I did mind them trying to make me unrecognizable by bleaching my hair or redoing my mouth or eyebrows. I had no *hope* of looking like Garbo, but even so they gave me her eyebrows and her hairdo. Awful!

Q: They also wanted you to become Bette *Davies*, right?

A: *Bettina Davies*, if you please! [*throws hands up*] Heaven forbid! And I would never have agreed to be Bette Davies, even, because I preferred my own name and there already was a Miss Davies, and I didn't want to be confused with anybody's mistress!

Q: Did you enjoy doing interviews, or avoid them?

A: I did them, of course. To some degree. Didn't usually enjoy them—the questions were often inane, especially for the ladies' magazines. "Do you love to cook your husband's favorite dishes? How do you keep your skin soft?" But if I was busy or overworked, I put my foot down and didn't do them. The worst were the prissy lady interviewers, the professional virgins who idolized Miss Hopper and Miss Parsons. These women were naive and judgmental at the same time. Dreadful creatures!

Q: "Professional virgins"?

A: Oh, yes—even if they'd had five children. And I would get asked to offer my favorite recipes, not my theories about acting or my views about anything. We were always prohibited by the studio publicists from giving our views on anything.

Q: Boy…did they call those women "sob sisters"?

A: Among other things! I remember a marvelous story about Tallulah Bankhead and one of the lady reporters. I don't know if it's true or not. She'd entertained this dreadful woman who'd made it quite clear that she didn't approve of Tallulah's lifestyle, but she kept smiling, then finally escorted the lady to the elevator and waited until she got into the crowded elevator. Then Tallulah waved to her as the doors shut, and she shouted, "Dahling, you're the nicest lesbian I've ever met!"

Q: [*both laugh*] That is good!

A: That is, or was, Miss Bankhead.

Q: Why are today's actors so dull, in comparison?

A: I don't know. Reporters ask me, but I don't know.…To paraphrase from *Sunset Boulevard*, "We had personalities then."

Q: Do you have any other Tallulah stories? After all, you knew her, didn't you?

A: We met occasionally at parties. This story is probably apocryphal, but they say Noel Coward was at one of her "mahvelous" parties, and he decided to leave early. The hostess begged him to stay, but he insisted, "I must think of my youth," and the frustrated hostess—and this is something Tallulah might very well say—she snapped, "Well, next time, bring him along!"

There's another one attributed to her, but it's rather naughty....

Q: I'm of age—despite my looks.

A: [*smiles*] Supposedly, Tallulah was reminiscing with an old actress friend of hers, and they'd been drinking a bit when the other actress fondly asked Tallulah, "Do you remember the minuet?" Tallulah said, "My dear, I can't even remember the men I *laid*." [*cackles with laughter*]

Q: [*after laughing*] There must be a million Tallulah stories, every one a gem.

A: Wait [*trying to recall*]. There is one more. Crude, but very Tallulah. Let's see....She was in the ladies' room, in a stall. And there was no toilet paper, so she bent down and asked the woman in the next stall, "Do you have any paper in there? I'm all out." The woman replied that she had none. Then Miss Bankhead asked, "Do you have any tissue in your purse?" and the woman, quite embarrassed, said no, she had none of that either.

So Tallulah finally asked, "Well, have you got two fives for a ten dollar bill?"

Q: Even the raunch was wittier then. Or so it seems. You do know that the great impressionist Charles Pierce does both you and Tallulah in his act?

A: [*drily*] So I understand. [*pause*] Who's more popular?

Q: You are! You are easily his most famous and frequent impression. [*she smiles indulgently*] You've never been to see his act? You should. It's not sloppily done and it's not malicious, although it's very bitchy.

A: Bitchy, I don't mind too much.

Q: He does other greats, like Hepburn, Crawford, Gloria Swanson as Norma Desmond [*in* Sunset Boulevard],...but you're the main attraction.

A: Are you his press agent?

Q: No, Miss D., I'm not. He's a real talent.

A: Well, I've never gotten around to going. But [*sarcastically*] I do appreciate your eye for talent.

Q: That's why I'm here, I guess. Do you find it uncomfortable to be imitated?

A: No, no. It *is* the sincerest form of flattery—outside of sex, of course!

Q: [*ignoring the attempt to change the subject*] Arthur Blake also did you very well, I heard, but he was before my time. Do you think men do the best Davis imitations?

A: Not always. There have been women who did me in their acts, and quite well. Of course, I've nevah taken it the wrong way. I'm not paranoid. Not like Mae West. She used to *sue.*

Q: Why would she feel so threatened?

A: Insecurity.

Q: That's sad. You know, Pierce also does Tallulah very well, and he does the two of you feuding. It's hilarious.

A: I've been told. But it's silly—we had no feud.

Q: It's been said she resented your making movies of her greatest stage triumphs. But she wasn't as big on screen, and the film versions were offered to you....

A: That is so right! As far as I'm concerned, there was no feud. A large percentage of my movies was based on wonderful Broadway plays. *She* was a stage actress, *I* was a film actress....What I find rather distasteful are the comments that Mr. Pierce insinuates Miss Bankhead had a crush on me.

Q: I've seen him a few times, and he doesn't state that. I think everyone knows by now that she was AC/DC. But he did make one amusing but suggestive comment—he said you were opening in a play somewhere and Tallulah sent you a congratulatory telegram that read "Kisses on your opening." He does so many quick little one-liners like that, and they're all in jest.

A: Such a jest *could* be construed as libelous [*Miss Davis meant slanderous*].

Q: Maybe we should get back to the forties. May I ask if Hollywood parties then were more glamorous than today?

A: My dear, everything was more glamorous then. Things didn't look so...standardized. Like the cars. A luxury car stood out then. And rich people didn't dress down, while secretaries couldn't afford copies of Dior, which at any rate didn't exist then. But I wasn't a partygoer. It has nothing to do with acting, and acting was then—as now—my life.

So I didn't go. When I do get together with my friends, it's intimate, *not* a big to-do.

Q: Another difference from today is that yesterday's movie stars looked like stars....

A: [*flicks her ashes into an ashtray and almost makes it*] Oh, today all they talk about is box office and ratings! Back then, you sometimes had an exchange of ideas, and all sorts of personalities. It was more fun. I didn't often go, but there was one party I'll never forget. It was at Ouida and Basil Rathbone's; everyone was beautifully dressed, the men too. It could be intimidating to a girl from New England. But I often did more listening than talking, especially before I established myself.

Q: Before you became a diva?

A: [*firmly smiling*] I *like* that word and, contrary to rumor, I have a perfectly pleasant singing voice. And I *have* recorded....Anyway, I was not yet thirty, and I distinctly remember perching myself on the arm of a big stuffed sofa. Two older actresses were sitting on it. To *me*, they seemed older; now, I'm not even sure if they'd be middle-aged. As I said, I was less than thirty. I was eating some canapés as one of the ladies said to the other, "Oh, I shudder to think of forty." I imagine she was in her mid-to-late thirties. But then the other actress responded, "Oh, what happened then?"

Well, it struck me as very funny, and I damn near choked on the canapé, and the two ladies looked up and gave me the dirtiest stare. But I've always remembered that, and I can tell you, *I* shuddered, when I reached forty.

Q: Aging's not what it's cracked up to be, eh?

A: It's only tolerable by comparison....

Q: To the alternative, yes. You know, several of your movies have been remade, among them *Dark Victory*—

A: At least they had the decency to change the title [*to* Stolen Hours *with Susan Hayward*].

Q: And even *The Letter*, but as a TV film. Have you viewed any of these?

A: No, and consequently I cannot offer any opinion on them, except that it is a grave mistake to try and remake them in the first place. [*pause*] Have you seen any of them?

Q: A few of the feature films. *Stolen Hours*, because Hayward was my mother's favorite actress. She was good in it, but it was very different from *Dark Victory*....Um, I saw George Cukor's version of *Old Acquaintance* [Rich and Famous *with Jacqueline Bisset and Candice Bergen*].

A: What did you think of it?

Q: It was so-so. I expected more, particularly from Cukor. But he didn't initiate the project—he took it over from another director, so it doesn't count as a true Cukor film.

A: Yes, George is a talent. A fine women's director.

Q: He hates that term.

A: I know. But after all these decades, he'd better get used to it!

Q: You're one of the few great actresses he didn't direct. Is that because he fired you from his theater group [*in Rochester, New York*]?

A: *I'm* the one who keeps stating that Mr. Cukor fired me. *He* doesn't talk about it.

Q: If I'm not mistaken, you were fired because, in his words, you had "no team spirit." Is that true?

A: No! On the other hand, and let's be frank about this, team spirit is for those who don't really aspire to much. Look at ballet: It's the corps de ballet that has the team spirit—not the prima ballerina.... [*smiles superiorly*] Speaking of Italian words, you must know that "prima donna" simply means "first lady," so it has no negative meaning at all.

Q: I guess the negative connotations were added by male chauvinists who disliked uppity actresses.

A: Yes, although "uppity" is not a word I care for. There is all the difference on earth between being negative for the sake of it—like Miriam Hopkins was—and being forceful, as I *had* to be, for the good of the product and for self-preservation.

Q: I have to admit to you that I've not yet seen *Old Acquaintance* with you and Hopkins. It's almost never on TV, and isn't available on videocassette.

A: What a shame. But just wait. This video business is a wonderful thing for those who do appreciate classic films. Now that television is turning its back on them.

Q: That's true, because there are more channels than ever, but I see fewer of your movies on, or those of Garbo, etc. I'm not sure why this is. Do you know?

A: Yech... [*grumbles inaudibly*] I don't know. Several reasons. Again, it is *ratings* that count to these juvenile executives, and apparently ratings decree that a movie with mass murder is more popular than a well-made human interest story. It is *junk*! They claim—and *I* do not believe it—that the Jerry Lewis pictures outdraw Garbo or me, so they put *him* on! But art is not ratings, it should have nothing to do with ratings, and now they have an *end*less backlog of made-for-television movies to show, and I suppose those are cheaper to show. They certainly look cheaper!

Q: You have made some fine telefilms.

A: Thank you, yes. And then, television is turning into an enemy of old movies, with this colorizing nonsense. So really, video is the only way to go, for the future.

Q: Several of your films are appearing on videocassette.

A: I'm glad. I am glad people are tiring of these mindless sit-coms and those night things like *Dallas* where all they do is hop into bed with anyone who's within spitting distance.

Q: Is it true that you publicly called the series *Hotel Brothel*? [*Davis had appeared on early episodes of the then-new series.*]

A: Absolutely true, and it should indeed have been called *Brothel.* They can't come up with good stories, so they substitute bodies in bed! If the writers can't come up with stories and good characters, then they should sell life insurance, and Mr. [*Aaron*] Spelling should hire brand-new writers.

Q: I guess the one positive thing about the nighttime soaps is they're bringing back some of the old glamour, right?

A: What do you mean?

Q: Shows like *Dynasty* showcase actresses like Joan Collins and Linda Evans, and they wear elegant clothes....

A: My dear, it takes more than draping a body in something expensive to create real glamour....Hah! What's elegant about all that cleavage? My God, they might as well be at the beach! I had a very good bust, and I never was costumed to resemble a streetwalker unless I was *playing* a streetwalker.

Q: What do you think of Joan Collins?

A: [*a frown, but no other response*]

Q: They say she's improved the status of actresses over fifty.

A: How? By playing a slut?

Q: Yet somewhere I read that her character, Alexis, is the sort that you used to play—a woman of great power who always gets her way.

A: *Please* don't say that. No, no, no. Whatever she is playing has nothing whatever to do with me or what I played, not with any of the roles I played. And you must remember that when I played a fallen woman, as in *The Letter*, she got punished in the end. They didn't make her richer, or glamorize it. No. I do not think much of Miss Collins's so-called allure.

Q: You worked together in the fifties....

A: Did we?

Q: *The Virgin Queen* [*in which Davis again played Elizabeth I*].

A: Oh, yes. She *was* in that, wasn't she? [*stubs out cigarette thoroughly*]

Q: I guess we'll change the subject.

A: [*brightly*] Let's.

Q: I know you've said the studio system was, overall, better for developing actors and creating stars. Is there anything about today's Hollywood that is an improvement?

A: Let me think....No. Just one thing. More money. Far more money. In fact, too much money!

Q: Ten years or so ago, when big stars were getting one million
dollars rather than ten or twenty times that, Glenda Jackson said that nobody is worth one million. Do you agree?

A: First, let me say this is not a case of sour grapes. It might
sound that way, but it is not. On the other hand, I still feel
that when a Bette Davis picture is shown or marketed for
profit, Bette Davis should receive some small remunera-
tion—at least!—for it. It was Mr. Reagan and others of his
ilk who saw to it that the producers kept all the gold. He
sold out his own peers for his personal political advancement, and he's been promoting the very wealthy, ever
since.

Q: A quick question: What do you think of Nancy Reagan?

A: A quick answer: I never do.

Q: Back to the question of whether a performer is worth one
million dollars per picture.

A: The answer is no, because it's utterly ridiculous, when
there is *still* so much poverty in our great country. In the
sixties, under the Democrats, there was a War On Want. In
the eighties, with the Republicans, poverty is being
allowed, and worse than that, it is allowed to spread. I am
not a socialist, but what you just said about twenty million
dollars for one star, *that* is *insane!*

Q: Shirley MacLaine once said that if producers were dumb
enough to give her one million dollars a movie—this was
in the sixties—she was not dumb enough to turn it down.

A: [*laughs*] I would have said the same! Yes, that's perfectly
reasonable. That was when Miss MacLaine still used her
common sense.

Q: Have *you* ever had an out-of-body experience?

A: [*a pause, then rolls her eyes*] Does giving birth count? [*giggles, then laughs throatily*] Out-of-body, indeed! More like out of one's mind!

Q: Besides the studio contract system, what are the biggest changes in moviemaking from the Golden Era to now?

A: You make me sound like an archaeologist. One huge difference is all this going off on location. I cannot think who it benefits, other than foreign economies. It certainly does not benefit the actors. As I said when I was sent to Egypt for that [*Agatha*] Christie film [Death on the Nile], in my day Jack Warner would have built Egypt and the Nile on the back lot for me. *So* much more convenient! Without all the heat, the flies, the terrible food, the natives, and the illnesses.

Q: Mentioning *Death on the Nile*, I heard that a few of your lines had later to be re-dubbed in Hollywood, due to audio difficulties in Egypt, and—

A: Well, there you are.

Q: —and that your lines, because somehow you were no longer available, were recorded either by Charles Pierce or actor Michael Greer, since they both do great impressions of you. [*she winces*] Is that true?

A: I don't know. I would certainly have been willing to loop my own lines, thank you. I cannot believe that story is true, although I know it has been making the rounds. If any of that happened, it did so without *my* being consulted about it.

Q: When I saw you in your one-woman show in which you toured the world, you gave the audience a lesson in how to "do" Bette Davis—with the manic cigarette-puffing, the rotating elbows, and the line "Petah, Petah, Petah!" You obviously have a great sense of humor about being burlesqued.

A: [*smiles*] Well, it *is* an honor. When you become very famous, as an actor or as a politician, they caricature you. And I'm perfectly aware that my caricature has nothing to do with any of my performances. For instance, I nevah said "Petah" in any movie. That's just a caricature. Who the hell *was* Petah? I don't even remember. But it happens, once you're very famous, and it's rather like a tax for being famous. I hope that I have accepted it gracefully.

Q: I remember when you appeared on the stage after the half-hour of film clips, you came out, looked the place over, put your fists on your hips, and spat, "What a dump!"

A: [*laughs fondly*] What else could I say? They'd nevah have forgiven me if I'd said, "Good evening," instead. They expect me to be on my worst behavior.

Q: We love it. But how does one accept critics and bad or personal reviews? Do you ever get used to it?

A: Well, that too, unfortunately, is a form of tax that one has to endure. The best policy is to *try* and ignore it, and to cut off the so-called friends who insist on bringing it up. And really, all that criticism is here today, then gone tomorrow. The critics are very temporary, sometimes very bitter, and no one remembers them. It is the body of work of an artist that matters, not what any self-appointed critic has said, however influential or widely read he or she may be at the moment.

Q: The German director Rainer Werner Fassbinder told me that for him critics are like eunuchs—they cannot do, and so they critique.

A: True. But one of those French writers that nobody in America remembers really hit the nail on the head. He was writing a letter to a critic who'd sent him a bad review. Now, this isn't the most tasteful thing in the world, but it makes a very relevant point. So the famous writer wrote back to the critic. He said, "I am sitting in the smallest room of my large house. I have your review before me. Soon, it will be behind me...."

Q: *Touché*, Miss Davis.

A: Very *touché*.

HER PRODUCER: DAVID LEWIS

I originally sought out producer David Lewis to interview him about director James Whale, the man behind *Frankenstein, Bride of Frankenstein, The Invisible Man, The Old Dark House, Waterloo Bridge* and *Showboat*. I'd been told merely that Lewis "knew" Whale, who took his life in 1957. That was the same year Lewis retired—his first film produced was *Camille* in 1936, his last *Raintree County* with Elizabeth Taylor and Monty Clift—for the two men had been lifemates.

Whale's directing career was ended when he refused to stop living with Lewis (né Levy). His last film was the aptly titled *They Dare Not Love*. Shorn of his career and prestige, and victimized by failing health, the flamboyant Brit jumped into his swimming pool in 1957. Lewis survived him by three decades, dying in 1987 in West Hollywood in his early eighties.

Lewis became a friend of mine after I first interviewed him in his small, overheated apartment in 1978. He began his producing career via Irving Thalberg at MGM, then moved to Warners when the homophobic Louis B. Mayer assumed complete control of MGM after Thalberg's premature death. At the Burbank-based studio, Lewis produced Ronald Reagan's best picture, *King's Row*, and Bette's best—in her own estimation—*Dark Victory*, plus the Davis vehicles *The Sisters, All This and Heaven Too* and *In This Our Life.*

BH: Was she easy to work with?

DL: Not by any stretch of the imagination! Garbo was a breeze, compared with her.

BH: But was it worth it, working with her?

DL: You have to work with somebody, and I preferred to work with a topflight star. Everyone did, for their career's sake. With Bette Davis, the end might be said to justify the means. The films I did with her were justified by critics and the public.

BH: Your producing was done in conjunction with Hal Wallis, wasn't it?

DL: Hal wasn't mad about the girl, either. He was a power at Warners, and so was Bette, whom they nicknamed the fifth Warner Brother. Once she had her power, she clung to it tenaciously. She and Hal had frequent scraps.

Years later, when Hal wrote his memoirs, he noted that his favorite of the actresses he'd worked with was Katharine Hepburn. Said she was the nicest, or the most civil. Bette was crushed! She sent me a note asking me why he'd said that and how could he do that to her! Bette wanted to be thought of as Miss Congeniality as well as the First Lady of the American cinema.

BH: Did you ever see her mistreat Wallis any more than another star player might have done?

DL: She would issue ultimatums, knowing that sometimes she would have to give in, though not usually. It was a way of flexing her muscles. She had to let everyone know that she was the sun, and they were her satellites.

BH: Do you think this carried over into her private life?

DL: I wasn't part of her inner circle. We were friendly during the Warner years, but by the time she left, she had alienated most of those she'd worked with. Bette knew about James and me, and she was friendly. She was even friendlier to Wallis, as he had more influence. But when she found out that James and I were pals with Crawford, Bette grew quite cool. Until many years later, when her friends from the glory days were dead, and she started reaching out in friendship.

BH: Is she somebody who needed an audience, in private life as well as public?

DL: I believe so. Most of her circle were those who would look up to her or were dependent on her in some way. Her relatives, her fans, her gentleman admirers and those celebrities who were willing to bask in her glow.

BH: What about her friend Olivia de Havilland?

DL: That's a good for instance. Olivia is in her own right a star, albeit a less colorful one than Bette. Olivia has two Oscars to Bette's two. Bette likes her and likes her company because they have that gilded past in common. But Olivia has learned—or rather she knew from the beginning—to play princess to Bette's queen. Bette Davis is proof positive that the wheel that squeaks loudest gets the grease.

BH: How do you think the Davis rambunctiousness affected her marriages?

DL: She once said to me that she's never met a man she could trust, genuinely trust. Whether that comes of being abandoned by her father early on...I think Bette views men as obstacles. She likes them, but she feels she has to somehow show her dominance. Since the last marriage ended, she's become more and more belligerent with men.

BH: Including interviewers and the press?

DL: Her career is where she lives. She wouldn't jeopardize that. She's said that her career is her, and she is her career. In my own career, I never met anybody as career-oriented as she is.

BH: It must be tough on her, not being Number One?

DL: She's no masochist. She knows. She's accepted reality. But now we've been losing touch, and that's a good sign, from her side of it. The sixties and seventies were a bad time for her—everyone dying, her own growing old, and those Gothic movies that almost made her a joke. But with the eighties, she's being taken up again and treated like the national treasure she is—as a performer, if not an individual!

BH: Do you like her?

DL: If I'm not in her cheering section, it's not because she's let our friendship slide a few times. You can't expect any genuine friendship or reciprocity from anyone in Hollywood who's making it. It's just that Bette Davis's only enduring loyalty is to the Davis career. She's mercurial—one minute she's thanking you for a gift, the next she's forgotten about it and is haranguing you for some imagined slight.

BH: Why did she cool toward you and James when she found out Joan was your friend?

DL: That should be obvious. It's competition. The stars are always in competition, and besides that, Bette was always out of sympathy with the type of actress who primps and preens, like Joan did. I think she had a slight inferiority complex toward the stars who made it on looks and who always looked, almost effortlessly, spectacular.

BH: It's funny to think Davis could have an inferiority complex about anything!

DL: Once she got older, she saw that she was fortunate. She was still in the running, while the pretty girls were fading or turning to flab. But at the time, at Warners, she was very conscious of not being a classical beauty, and several people around her said she didn't want to be in the same room with Joan, because people would compare them.

BH: Yet she later walked all over Joan Crawford.

DL: Bette covers her real feelings with bluster. She knew she could whip any clotheshorse into line. Bette fights like a man—ruthlessly. But you have to hand it to her. She battled Hollywood and won, and she's proven that an actress of substance outlasts an actress of surface appeal....

BH: Summing up, then, how would you say Bette Davis differed from all the rest?

DL: I think she's always put her career first—always. I think she is the only star, male or female, of whom that can truly be said.

THE *M* EN

A: You want to talk about the *men* in my life?! Hah! *This* should be juicy!

Q: One can only hope, Miss Davis…

A: [*shakes head dubiously and lights up cigarette*] I *could* get to like you, Boze! Just be careful what you ask. This is a touchy subject.

Q: One of your frequent leading men during your Warners heyday was George Brent. He was a star then. Why isn't he much remembered today?

A: …Well, George worked mostly at Warners. He was one of those handsome, competent actors whom housewives could fantasize about. He wasn't talented or exceptional enough—like Bogart, if you like—to become a major star. He knew this. Once, he told me during a drunken moment at a party, "Bette, I envy you. You're so special, while I'm ordinary."

Q: One reviewer called him a second-rate Ronald Colman.

A: To me, he was more than that. Nor did I find Mr. Colman all that fascinating.

Q: He hasn't held up as well as some.

A: Mr. Colman had a voice. Voices were highly esteemed then. Today, I doubt that would be enough.

Q: You had an [*well-documented*] affair with Mr. Brent?

A: Who said so? [*defensively*] I *nevah* said that. I did fall in love with him....

Q: Was he typical of most leading men, that is, trying to bed his leading ladies?

A: In those days, George could afford to be picky. You see, he was a snob. I worked with him before my real stardom, and he paid me little attention. But once I was a star, he suddenly became very interested. I believe that he only liked to go to bed with stars. An ego thing [*smiles*].

Q: Was he reputed to be a good lover, or just a frequent one?

A: ...He was a very good lover. In fact, I am sure he was a much better lover than a husband. He married five times. Two of the wives were women I worked with—Ruth Chatterton and Ann Sheridan. But his marriages were even briefer than mine [*shakes head disapprovingly*].

Q: I know he retired from films early. Was it because he hadn't become a topnotch star?

A: [*ignoring first part of question*] He really didn't get a chance to shine at Warners, because he often played dull but necessary roles. Like the heroine's husband or fiancé. The women's parts were *so* well-written then, you see. What we did were women's pictures, and those were big box office. Today, they use it as a name for *specialized* pictures, which is idiotic, since women are over half the audience! So, poor George must have tired of usually being merely decorative.

I know that he resented his leading ladies quite a bit.

Q: Do you think that had something to do with his—pardon my English—wanting to screw them so much?

A: [*laughs*] It could be! I never thought of that.

Q: He did have some good roles, like your doctor in *Dark Victory*. But he retired in the mid–1950s and then did one more role in a flop movie of the late 1970s.

A: I remember. He did it shortly before he died. George died of emphysema. Everyone was always telling *me* to beware of that dread disease! I never listened. And then I heard a joke on television which one of those myriad impersonators of mine did, and it expressed exactly how I feel....

Q: You weren't scared of lung cancer?

A: [*irritably*] I have a private list of things I am afraid of. Cancer is not high on that list.

Q: What was the impersonator's joke?

A: He said, as *me*, "I just returned from my doctor's. [*she does a Bette Davis impression, waving her hand with a cigarette in it*] He told me that for every cigarette you smoke, you lose one minute of your life.... I asked, 'Doctor, what does that *mean*?' And he said, 'It means you died twenty years ago." Hah! [*roars with laughter*]

Q: Like the song says, you're still here....

A: Damn right! About dear George Brent, poor thing, he took

that final little role as a favor to Irving Rapper, who directed the movie. Irving had directed some of my best pictures [*including* Now, Voyager].

Q: You said Brent was an alcoholic?

A: Oh, yes. Chronic. But it didn't interfere with his work, so I do not judge him.

Q: You worked twice with the veddy English Leslie Howard, who in reality was a Jewish-Hungarian, as was Douglas Fairbanks, Sr.

A: Believe it or not.

Q: He was your leading man in your breakthrough movie, *Of Human Bondage*, also the star of *The Petrified Forest*, which made a leading villain of Bogart.

A: Yes, Bogey adored Leslie. He was so grateful to him, because he'd been dying to become famous, and it was all thanks to Leslie. So when he had a son, he named him Leslie. We all got a chance to shine in Leslie's films. Today, he is not so highly regarded—he comes across rather wooden. Perhaps he tried too hard to be completely English.

Q: Even in *Pygmalion*, he seems stiff. Was he easy to work with?

A: Yes…and no. [*frowns*] He was very much the big star, very important. Yet he did not like strong women. Strong actresses, in particular. When we did *Bondage*, he knew that as Mildred I would walk away with the acting honors. He did get to play a cripple, and he got all the audience sympathy, which in those days everyone craved—*I* did not. But he knew I would steal the show, and his fear of me and my role caused him to be less than friendly towards me!

Q: Did that hurt you, or matter much?

A: Not at all. I knew what would happen for me. Well, pretty much, for I *was* taking a real risk. I would either be booed out of Hollywood by audiences who detested Mildred, or I would finally be recognized as a dramatic actress. So really, Mr. Howard's iciness was of no consequence. If anything, it was helpful for my character, who looked down on him. If we had been fond of each other in real life, I'd have had to have worked harder to act contemptible towards him.

Q: When you later worked with him, he was quite friendly to Bogart, I've read. But Bogart had the showier role....

A: Yes. A strange man, Mr. Howard.

Q: Known to be both a great lover and quite, um—

A: Well-hung, as they say. Yes.

Q: That's what I was trying to say. Did you hear the rumor that his female private secretary was really his lover?

A: We all heard that one! I don't know if it was true. She, of course, could have been both! There were also many rumors that his favorite activity was oral sex, and that his secretary, shall we say, catered to him....

Q: That must have been a dynamite rumor, then.

A: It was. In those days, that type of sex was definitely considered unnatural.

Q: Would a rumor like that harm a heterosexual actor's career?

A: Probably not. Not unless the public became aware of it, and *no* newspaper would have published a story like *that*.

Q: I beg to differ. When Chaplin was divorced by one of his wives—

A: [*smirking*] His child brides!

Q: Right. This particular wife cited as a complaint that he'd had her fellate him, and the papers printed it.

A: Really?

Q: You didn't know that? I'm surprised, because it was a *cause célèbre*, though of course it was in the twenties, so before your time....

A: [*mollified*] Yes, besides which it was a matter of record, which is why the papers ran the story.

Q: Naturally, they used the Latin term for it [*fellatio*], and most people had never heard or read the word.

A: Nowadays, even children know [*shakes head*].

Q: How, then, would you characterize Leslie Howard?

A: ...A cold fish.

Q: He didn't put the make on you?

A: No. Remember that a man like that would prefer a very pliable female.

Q: A noncompetitor?

A: Yes. [*wryly*] A girl who would gladly get on her knees to him.

Q: Moving right along, uh...What about Errol Flynn? He was renowned for being a Lothario.

A: You mean did he make a pass at me? [*smiles*] I was not his type, alas. He went after dear Olivia [*de Havilland*], who had a tremendous crush on him.

Q: From what we know of his rape trials, he—like Chaplin— preferred teenagers.

A: Oh, he liked young girls, all right, but I'm sure Errol would have screwed anything that moved.

Q: Apparently he had some male flings too. Truman Capote, for one, admitted he'd worshipped at his shrine.

A: Hmm. I heard about him and Ty Power. That may have been just curiosity. Errol was basically heterosexual. He liked women. Or should I say that he liked sex with women, because Errol really had no high regard for women. Quite the contrary. He abused them often.

Q: Do you think the so-called Don Juan complex is sometimes based on contempt for women?

A: I do think that. It may be more difficult for some men to love one woman and be nice to her than to bed a thousand women....But Errol had many sides to his complex personality. He was not, I am sorry to say, a nice man, though I'm not the first to say or reveal this.

Q: One of his biographers claimed that Flynn was a secret Nazi, or a Nazi spy.

A: [*laughing*] I find it difficult to imagine Errol had the brains to be a spy. Or the courage. He was definitely a me-first type of fellow. A Nazi sympathizer, that I unfortunately don't doubt. Errol was very racist and anti-Semitic. Everybody knew that—he always talked that way, and dared you to disapprove of it. He was always calling Jack Warner a "dirty Jew," a "kike" and other names. Not a nice man at all!

Q: I read Flynn was also a slave trader.

A: I would not put it past him!

Q: And his drinking bouts were legendary.

A: Mr. Warner had terrible trouble with him all the time, with his drinking on the set. That is what I really had against Errol Flynn. He was not a professional. And at the time, even though he was popular with the public and women adored his looks, in our business he was something of a joke. All good looks, and not much else.

Q: The story goes that Warner wanted to star you and Flynn in *Gone With the Wind*, and you declined the role of Scarlett O'Hara because Flynn would be Rhett Butler. True?

A: Well, Jack Warner was not the best at casting. He would have cast Flynn as Butler if he could have gotten away with it. Happily, American readers said that only Gable could play the role.

Q: Yet Gable was himself no great actor.

A: No, but he *was* Rhett Butler.

Q: And he didn't even affect a Southern accent, or try to.

A: He didn't need to, and he was American, as opposed to Errol, who was from Australia. The thing is, audiences sometimes don't want you to act *too* much; this is more true of actors than actresses.

Q: Vivien Leigh, who played Scarlett, was English.

A: She *had* to become the character, whereas Clark did not. You see, even in acting, women are expected to do more....But anyway, I did not look forward to working with Flynn a second time—and you forgot that I did *another* picture with Leslie Howard, called *It's Love I'm After*. We played an acting couple like the Lunts, and originally it was titled *Gentleman After Midnight*.

All right. Now, about Errol: In 1938, I did a picture with him, *The Sisters*. And Errol was a big star in Hollywood, from his first picture. He was billed above me. But they wanted to bill him above the title, alone. I fought that. After *Jezebel*, I felt I had a right to be billed above the title.

I also thought that "Errol Flynn in *The Sisters*" had certain sexual connotations....And I won my fight. We were *both* billed over the title, and I was pleased to be in a film with him, because he was box office and it helped me.

Q: But a year or so later, you came to do *The Private Lives of Elizabeth and Essex*, and you were ace box office yourself....

A: Yes. Among other things, I had done *Dark Victory*, a really big jewel in my crown. And *this* was a historical story, and I very much wanted Laurence Olivier for Essex. Flynn was just not talented enough to play him. He wasn't English enough, he wasn't professional enough. Added to that problem, the studio had asinine ideas about the title. They wanted to hide that it was historical, and worse, they wanted to shift the emphasis to *his* role. But *I* was the queen, and he just a nobleman.

So, again, I had to go to war with Mr. Warner.

Q: You won....

A: For the most part. The film was from a play titled *Elizabeth the Queen*. In that era you, of course, could not have used the expression "virgin queen" because of "virgin." Essex was in on the title of the picture, but I insisted Elizabeth's name come first, and in the end I think I really did win, because I received the acting honors, and it is now one of my cherished pictures—a classic, of course.

Q: I have a photocopy here from the *New York Times*. The reviewer wrote, "Bette Davis's Elizabeth is a strong, resolute, glamour-skimping characterization against which Mr. Flynn's Essex has about as much chance as a beanshooter against a tank."

A: [*beams hugely*] Well, then!

Q: Is it true you once had a run-in with Victor McLaglen?

A: [*smiles majestically*] Another forgotten actor. No, not really a run-in—he was very tall, terribly tall. A tall *actor*, he was not....I did hold my tongue, so there was no run-in. After all, a tongue can be a lethal weapon. What happened is very simple; it was blown out of all proportion.

Q: [*I refrain from saying, "Unlike Mr. Howard."*] What happened?

A: We won Academy Awards in 1935. He was Best Actor for *The Informer*, I Best Actress for *Dangerous*, although of course I was given the Oscar for *Of Human Bondage*, from the year before—as you must know.

Q: Not only that, I know that in 1934, when you weren't even nominated for Mildred in *Bondage*, a write-in vote was accepted for the first time.

A: [*impressed*] This is why I like talking to you and even answering some of your more forward questions—you don't ask me things you should already know!

Q: That would make it dull for you. And frightening for me.

A: [*smiles*] Ah, yes. Now. Victor McLaglen. [*frowns*] All that happened was that I went to accept my award wearing a simple but pleasant dress. Mr. McLaglen whispered to me, "You musta decided to come as a housewife." Which I thought most impertinent, but I held my tongue. Barely!

Q: What did you *feel* like saying?

A: Oh, something on the order of, "You're smarter than you look." Because, you know, although he was English, you'd never have guessed it. He played bum types.

Q: But then you soon won a second Oscar, to his one....

A: [*smiling*] Well, revenge is never my motive for anything. However I did pay heed to *others'* criticism of my dress. My "bad" dress! [*laughs*] The movie magazine editors told me that housewives across the country expected glamour from an actress, and they had a point, for it was still the Great Depression. The next time I won, I wore feathers, and went partly uncovered. Nobody complained, and I'm sure Mr. McLaglen was by then wishing that he was getting roles as good as I was.

Q: In your opinion, does a woman dress for other women, or for men?

A: I dress for *me*, above all. To be quite frank. But I do hold with the saying that women dress for each other but undress for their men!

Q: Would you agree that the extreme of the ever well-dressed and coiffed star was Joan Crawford?

A: You mean those stories that she wouldn't even go to the market without dressing to the nines?

Q: Yes. Looking like a *star*, as she often said.

A: It's all right—if you want to be that self-conscious.

Q: She once explained that Louis B. Mayer, during her MGM days, had instilled that in her.

A: It's logical. Metro had that air of unreality, while Warners was a pioneer in social realism. So I didn't have that pressure to appear as if I'd landed from a Paris fashion show.

Q: Did you ever make the best-dressed lists?

A: I don't know. I never concerned myself with that. Certain actresses loved to talk endlessly about clothes, hairdos and their jewelry. I avoided them like the plague.

Q: Who, for instance?

A: I shouldn't name names.

Q: Why not?

A: ...Loretta Young, to name only one. [*pause*] God, I'd hate to have her last name. What happens when you get *old*?

Q: She could legally change it....

A: [*laughs, then coughs*]

Q: I have a confession to make about Ms. Crawford.

A: [*wary*] Oh-oh...

Q: I was foolish enough to pass up a chance to meet her. It's a long story. I could have gone to her New York apartment, but someone was there that I didn't wish to encounter. Now, I could kick myself.

A: And *I* could *kiss* you! [*a smiling, appraising pause*] I *knew* I liked you.

Q: Let's talk some more about Hollywood men. Like the great photographer George Hurrell....

A: He was at Warners only a few years, I believe, but he took hundreds and hundreds of photos of me. More than any other Warners star. What did he say about me?

Q: He said you had an innate ability to turn your moods on and off, a real asset for a photographic subject. That the shots he took of you as Judith Traherne in *Dark Victory* [*1939*] are among the best portrait studies of you ever.

A: Also among my most vulnerable, did he say?

Q: That's right. He said he felt that when you were playing Judith you were undergoing a great turmoil in your personal life, and that it helped your performance. He didn't dare ask you about your personal life....

A: I kept it very much apart from people at the studio, however much I liked them.

Q: May one inquire what was going on with you in 1939?

A: You may, but I won't answer. George was right—it was quite a bad time for me. I was quite unhappy, for a while.

Q: Was it a man?

A: I won't say.

Q: Did you consciously use your inner anguish to help your performance?

A: I use everything at my command when I act. Which is not to say that it was Method acting, which wasn't even called that yet.

Q: You're not an advocate of the Method, I take it.

A: You can take the Method too. To me, acting is something you do. You don't talk and whine endlessly about it or write books on how to do it or make a career out of teaching it. You act simply by acting, and to me, the best acting method is *good* acting!

Q: My favorite quote on the subject involves Laurence Olivier, whom you championed before Hollywood did [*she smiles*] and before Hollywood went overboard and canonized him [*she nods*]. He was making *Marathon Man* with Dustin Hoffman for [*director*] John Schlesinger—

A: Oh, I loved [*his*] *Sunday, Bloody Sunday!* Great writing and great roles—I really envied Glenda Jackson.

Q: Yeah, and Peter Finch. So, one day Hoffman came to the set, and he looked terrible, because he hadn't slept all night. Olivier asked him why, and Hoffman said it was because he had to play a scene where he was supposed to be very sleepy and tired. Olivier said, "Couldn't you *act* it?"

A: [*throws head back, laughing*] Totally, totally true!

Q: Why haven't you worked for some of the newer directors like Schlesinger or Spielberg or even Bergman?

A: [*quietly*] They haven't asked me.

Q: That's a shame. Maybe they imagine you're above it all.

A: Well, if you know them or have any connections—and I mean this—tell them I'm not above *any*thing, except retirement.

Q: You never had a feud with an actor as legendary as the one with Crawford, did you?

A: I did *not* feud with her!

Q: You didn't like her, did you?

A: Hated her guts, but we did not feud at all.

Q: Yet it was an adversarial relationship?

A: ...I resisted her machinations. And she had an adversarial relationship with *life*, for God's sake!

Q: You were quoted as saying, "There may be a heaven, but if Joan Crawford is there, I'm not going."

A: [*smiles with guilty pleasure*] Would *you*?

Q: What made her so hard?

A: Her attitude. You can't blame anything or anyone else. *We* create our personalities, and it's no use complaining about a bad childhood, because once you're an adult, you run your own life, or *should.*

Q: You sound almost like Katharine Hepburn.

A: Oh, God! I'd rather look like her than sound like her! She sounds more and more like Donald Duck.

Q: Miss Davis, who were the best actors you worked with, or the ones most instrumental to your career advancement?

A: That's easy! The best actor I worked with was almost without doubt Claude Rains. A giant talent.

Q: Yet not a popular favorite.

A: Because he wasn't handsome or beautiful, and his warmth was a sometime thing. He was also from England—James Whale, the director, brought him over here to do the voice of *The Invisible Man*. *Wonderful* voice! A lovely man, and yes, just so wonderful to work with.

But the actor who was most important to my career was definitely George Arliss. Now, he was not only no beauty,—he made Claude look good! Mr. Arliss, whom everybody called *Mr.* Arliss, looked quite horsey.

Q: Why was he so important to you?

A: He had enormous prestige. He did very [*high*] quality pictures, and he was actually big box office. I was in a picture with a friend of his who recommended me to Mr. Arliss. Then I was in Mr. Arliss's *The Man Who Played God*, in 1932, and I worked with him again, and he talked me up to the brothers Warner, feeling very strongly that I should be in *Of Human Bondage*.

Q: He must have been a kind man.

A: He was an elderly man, and he could afford to be kind. Youth is the time of selfishness, and besides, Mr. Arliss was interested in good acting. He believed in talent, and I was and am eternally grateful.

Q: I've never seen him in a movie.

A: He was a silent star, then he had a run of hits in the 1930s. But I believe he retired from films in that decade, then died some time in the 1940s. His pictures are very rarely shown, which is a pity. His biggest hit, of course, was as Disraeli, whom he played twice in pictures, and the second time, he won the Oscar. The story goes that he was so famous as

Disraeli that in London two American lady tourists were seen in front of a statue of Prime Minister Disraeli, and one woman said to the other, "Look dear. They've put up a statue of George Arliss!" [*laughs*]

Q: It's nice to hear there were stars willing to help a deserving newcomer.

A: There really were...I worked with Lionel Barrymore, and he was helpful in a different way. He kept giving them negative advice—don't do this, don't do that. Then he came up with a quote which became very famous in this town. He said, "Half the people in Hollywood are dying to be discovered. The other half are afraid they will be."

Q: A quote as relevant today as ever! You never worked with Brando, but I seem to recall a photo of you two at the Academy Awards. Did you like him?

A: Gorgeous creature! Yes, very much.

Q: But since the 1950s, he's been the first star to consistently put down acting.

A: That is stupid. *If* he believes what he's saying. Remember that many actors say ridiculous things for the effect or publicity.

Q: Why do you think he would disparage acting?

A: I don't know, unless he is one of those gentlemen who think it's not a masculine profession. Spencer Tracy was always saying that.

Q: Then why not find another, less lucrative profession?

A: Hear, hear!

Q: Long, long ago, you co-starred with Doug Fairbanks, Jr. What was he like as an actor?

A: Milquetoast, I'm afraid. As an actor and a personality. He improved with age—age can be fine for a male actor, it can add some depth or interest. Mr. Fairbanks is a gentleman and well-liked, but he nevah had what it took for true stardom.

Q: He was the first example of the son of a star getting into movies.

A: A deplorable practice! Acting is not in the genes, and I feel nepotism is terrible and most unfair. It [acting] is an inherent talent which one develops, and it's difficult enough to gain a foothold as an actor without competition from stars' untalented offspring!

Q: I'm not crazy about actors' kids whose interviews always bemoan the alleged trials of having rich and famous parents with great connections.

A: Ditto.

Q: Fairbanks married Crawford when he was nineteen—she was older.

A: Of course.

Q: Hard to imagine those two as a couple....

A: She probably ate him for breakfast! *Not* in today's sense of the word...though, come to think of it....

Q: Now who's being naughty? [*both laugh*] You've co-starred with British actors like Michael Redgrave and Alec Guinness. How different are they from American actors?

A: Not much. Not as actors. As people? [*winks*] More of them are gay or openly bisexual or whatever. Redgrave was [*bisexual*]. I know, because he used to discuss his affair with Noel Coward! I couldn't believe it!

Q: That's interesting, because Coward, who was homosexual, didn't talk about it freely.

A: I *think* Guinness is heterosexual—appearances can be deceiving, with the British....Perhaps I shouldn't call him a bore. For, he *is* talented. He can play an entire family of characters. And when *we* worked together, I got the impression that he would have preferred to do a solo! He was nevah rude, but he's rather an iceberg. Of course, he nevah became a Hollywood star because he, too, was a milquetoast.

Q: How was Charles Boyer, your co-star in the memorable *All This and Heaven Too* [1940]?

A: Then, he was a sex symbol. Women would simply swoon, but *I* didn't see it. He had nice eyes, but beyond that...[*shrugs*] another iceberg, and perhaps the most vain man I ever worked with. Terribly serious about his looks. A wig, a corset, lifts in his shoes, and so on. When he took all that off, he must have looked like the Pillsbury Doughboy!

Q: You know whose personality I liked? William Powell.

A: A very big star. He lived to be quite old, didn't he?

Q: Yes, after retiring long before. He was best known as *The Thin Man*, but to me he's *Mr. Peabody and the Mermaid*.

A: Who was the mermaid?

Q: Ann Blyth. Perfect in the role.

A: Wasn't she the one in [*Crawford's*] *Mildred Pierce*?

Q: Yes, as a totally different character.

A: I remember—she was Joan's treacherous daughter... [*smirks*].

Q: Ironic that Crawford often played good mothers with bad daughters.

A: When reality was the other way around!

Q: You co-starred with Powell. Was he the perfect gentleman we were led to believe he was?

A: Oh, he had charm! He was suave. But he also had a big mouth and quite a sexual appetite.

Q: Wasn't he engaged to Jean Harlow?

A: [*nods*] One of the town's biggest skirt-chasers. [*laughs*] It's never the ones you think. Half the time, the ones you think, are gay. But Powell had as many women as any of the so-called studs. Another deceptive one was Walter Pidgeon....

Q: Walter Pidgeon? You're kidding.

A: Ask around. It's true.

Q: I believe you. It's just that—

A: It's just that it's nevah the ones you think. And very rarely the sex symbols, male or female.

Q: They used to say Marilyn Monroe was frigid.

A: That's what I mean. And apart from Powell, Jean Harlow didn't seem to get much satisfaction in her boudoir.

Q: In her boudoir, eh? I wonder how people could *know* Marilyn was frigid?

A: Perhaps she said so herself. By the fifties and sixties, the talk was becoming pretty free. In the 1930s and forties, we didn't dare comment on sex, or even mention the word!

Q: But if a woman doesn't *say* she's frigid—and who would?—how could it be known to be so?

A: There is truth in that. And I think a good many of the

ladies men label as being frigid might be other than het-
erosexually inclined.

Q: I'm sure many are. I mean, what's the male equivalent of
frigid? Or are all men hot to trot?

A: I think all men are. Some exceptions, possibly.

Q: Like Mr. Arliss? He gave that impression.

A: Impressions mean little, and neither does age. Men are
peculiar—they can be eighty-plus and still be grabbing!
[*shakes head*]

Q: Peter Lawford. You worked with him, and he'd been a sex
symbol to the bobby-soxers....

A: Most men in our business age well, or used to. Now they
don't mind getting fat young. But Peter *really* let himself
go. He got bloated, and he lost his charm and most of his
career, all from becoming involved with booze and drugs.
He was also, I often heard, one of the double-gaited ones.

Q: The what?

A: [*a stereotypical limp wrist indicating bisexuality*]

Q: Oh. Well, Sal Mineo told me that. He said they had an
affair together.

A: That I did not know. Yes, Sal was a sweet boy. I met him.
But the one who informed me about Peter first was
Keenan Wynn. Keenan, who is now deceased, went either
way—you know about his affair with Van Johnson, of
course?—and he was *very* close to Peter for a while. Peter's
mother once threw Keenan Wynn out of the house, and
Peter too. [*leans forward urgently*] Of course this is *not* for
publication while I am alive. Or Peter.

Q: But Peter Lawford is dead.

A: Oh, that's right. Well...[*shrugs*].

Q: How was Gary Merrill as an actor?

A: He was good within his range. A personable, forceful leading man. Perhaps he came to it too late to gain real popularity. He was good in action films—like *Twelve O'Clock High*.

Q: I didn't know until I read Merrill's book [*published in 1988*] that he liked to wear skirts, for comfort. How did you feel about that?

A: It was just an idiosyncrasy he had. He doesn't do it all the time. It is strictly for comfort, like the Scotsmen.

Q: I've been to Scotland in different seasons, and it's always cold—same latitude as Moscow—so I don't know what they find "comfortable" about kilts!

A: [*grinning*] Perhaps they like the updraft.

Q: By the way, Merrill's book's dedication reads, "Dedicated to all the children of the world...including Gore Vidal." Do you know why?

A: Well, I doubt they were lovers. Gary is completely hetero. I have no idea.

Q: Vidal, one of my favorite writers, wrote some of your movies—*The Catered Affair, The Scapegoat*. Might that have had anything to do with it?

A: No, no. They may share political sympathies. In which case, the three of us do.

Q: Make that the four of us! So much for that. Let me look over my notes....You said William Powell had a big mouth. What did you mean?

A: I was contrasting your image of him as a perfect gentle-

man with his being outspoken—by very few. He did
some pictures with Kay Francis, who was a major star in
her day, which was before my time, and then he went
around telling anyone who would listen that she *must* be
a good actress, because she played convincing love scenes
with *men*.

Q: He wasn't discreet.

A: In that era, such talk could be extremely damaging.

Q: So she was lesbian? I knew that she had to hide her
Judaism, or thought she had to.

A: Oh, religion was taboo, especially if it wasn't Christian. But
what I heard, elsewhere, was that Miss Francis had girlfriends, but only in between husbands....

Q: "Double-gaited."

A: Or in the mood for a change.

Q: I often wonder if women don't occasionally get fed up with
men?

A: I'm sure most every woman does! [*laughs*]

Q: You have?

A: Of course.

Q: Ever to Miss Francis's extent?

A: Hah! That is a ridiculous question, because even if it happened only once in a lifetime, who would ever admit to it?

Q: Today's generation?

A: *Only* today's generation!

Q: Powell must have been upset with Francis if he did say she
was bi or lesbian...?

A: She got into trouble, and plenty of it, without his loose lips.

Q: Like what?

A: I thought you would surely know. You know so much

about Warners in the 1930s....This was the mid-thirties. Miss Francis was the top-paid star there. Then, out of the blue, it was announced she would complete her contract by starring in B-pictures! It was simply unprecedented, and no reason was ever given. A huge embarrassment for such a star—she had many, many fans.

Q: Was there a scandal?

A: It wasn't permitted to evolve into a scandal, the studio saw to that. They saved her reputation, and everything was terribly hush-hush. They made you feel it wasn't even decent to gossip about it. But it all boiled down to another woman—in *her* boudoir. Jack Warner was despicable to Miss Francis. I felt awfully sorry for her, and it certainly scared every actress in town.

Q: Another case of the "morals" clause strikes again. Did Kay Francis ever explain it off?

A: She said what she had to: that she was looking forward to retiring. Or at least taking time off after having worked so hard. No one dared question her explanation, but it was known.

Q: I'm really amazed I never heard this; I grew up so close to Hollywood. So, Powell's comments didn't have anything to do with Francis being downgraded?

A: No, but the point is one shouldn't go around making statements which can hurt someone's career.

Q: Today it's debatable whether they could hurt, but then it was a fact that they did.

A: Anything out of the ordinary was potentially damaging. If one was revealed to be living in sin—

Q: To coin a tacky expression.

A: Or to be of partly colored ancestry....Times have changed a lot, sometimes for the better.

Q: In most cases. Miss Davis, are there any other actors you care to comment on?

A: No, I think you've been quite thorough!

Q: Then what would you say are the biggest differences between actors and actresses?

A: Besides the obvious one or ones, I think everything depends on the individual's personality. Overall, though, I think *actors* are more insecure and not as openly emotional, so therefore not as prepared to flesh out a character. They are also at least as vain as actresses. In one sense, I'm much more like an actor—I nevah considered retiring.

There are several actresses, some were stars, from the era when I began. These ladies retired at forty or forty-five. They usually stayed retired, much as they may have missed it. But some made a little comeback in a film or something on television. *That* sort of actress. Of course, if one takes years off, the career is bound to lose momentum, and you cannot regain it. There are several sad examples.

Q: Like Audrey Hepburn?

A: That's one. But as I was saying, my career wasn't based on something that is gone by forty. On the contrary, when I passed forty, I got a new lease on life—I got to play Margo Channing! Finally, *today*, actresses have come around to *my* attitude, which is that acting is for all your whole life long. And that we only get *better* at it!

HER CO-STAR: PETER LAWFORD

*M*id-1980. The Cafe of the Pink Turtle at the Beverly Wilshire Hotel. A luncheon interview for British *Photoplay* with transplanted Brit, Peter Lawford. At fifty-six, he looks older, even ravaged, and his manner alternates between embarrassingly attentive and absent-minded. Because he declines to speak about his private life, we discuss some of his better movies—"I only wish there were more of them to talk about!"

Lawford is affable, but uses occasional four-letter descriptions for less fondly remembered co-stars. Once a leading man, he is acutely aware that most interest now centers not on him but on the stars he supports. Like Davis. At one point, he elaborately shrugs, "Look, I'm bone-lazy. I wouldn't *want* to spend two months on *any* film."

BH: The inevitable question: What was it like to make love to Bette Davis [*in* Dead Ringer, *1964*]?

PL: [*laughs long and loud, turning heads in the restaurant*] I closed my eyes and thought of England! Or Marilyn Monroe. In point of fact, Bette's a good kisser.

BH: Tell me if I have this right. You played the kept man of the rich twin whom the poor twin murders, then she tries to fool you and everyone else that she's the rich twin?

PL: A passing grade! You win. [*laughs*] But then my character finds out she's an impostor; because she's frigid, unlike the rich, murdered twin. So he blackmails her.

BH: And you're killed when her giant dog rips you apart?

PL: On the nose. You have a vivid memory.

BH: Was it fun working with Miss Davis?

PL: Much to my chagrin, she was very pleasant. I expected the untamable shrew, and she was a nice, elderly lady who smiled at most everybody.

BH: A big contrast from a few years before, when she'd worked with Joan Crawford....

PL: Crawford puts everybody on edge. *Past* tense. I don't want to speak ill of the dead, but my associations with Joan Crawford were mercifully brief, and vinegary.

BH: Of course, on *Dead Ringer* the director was Bette's old friend and former co-star Paul Henreid.

PL: Paul's a gent. A European gent. Say, which is he, German or Austrian? I'm never clear on that.

BH: I believe he's Austrian.

PL: It was clear Bette trusted him. That counts for a hell of a lot, with Bette or any star. On that yucky *Baby Jane*, the guy in charge [*the director*] was fat old Bob Aldrich [*who also helmed* Hush, Hush, Sweet Charlotte]. Bob has the charisma and appeal of a soggy potato. Bette didn't know him, and he'd already worked with Joanie [*on* Autumn Leaves]. So Bette's paranoia was turned up full blast, and she half-suspected Aldrich and Joanie of having had an affair. Together!

BH: And therefore that he might favor Crawford with more close-ups and so forth?

PL: You got it. It was a heavy-tension set, and as a producer, I know about sets. I've been on more sets than I can count, hanging around or just playing producer, which mostly means looking rich. I'm *not*, but I *look* it!

BH: You produced *The Patty Duke Show*, didn't you?

PL: Yup. Which brings to mind a little Davis story. One of our writers thought to have Bette on as a guest star, but before he went ahead with a script, I had one of our people check into her availability. She wasn't doing much of anything, but she wanted all kinds of dough. Money, star treatment, perks—the works. Hey, it rhymes! So we scrapped the idea.

BH: That tallies with what I heard about Lucille Ball and Desi Arnaz trying to get Davis on their show [*Davis was Ball's favorite actress*]. She reportedly wanted too big a salary, so they got Tallulah Bankhead in her place, then wished they'd spent the extra money when Bankhead's drinking kept delaying their shooting schedule.

PL: For my money, Bankhead is no Davis substitute. Bankhead's best scenes were always offstage. Bette's best in front of a camera.

BH: You mean she's more exciting as a performer than a person?

PL: Yup. *Dead Ringer*, she was this anxious-seeming elderly lady with the wig and the roles of a couple of twins about ten years younger than herself. But she pulled it off. The lady is capable! That fire you see when she's on-camera, that wasn't there when she was just hanging around the set.

BH: She's known for her energy, isn't she?

PL: Sometimes. I mean, maybe the lady's schizophrenic. Maybe she's A on one set and Z on another. But on *Dead Ringer*, she seemed relieved to be putting herself into the hands of an old friend. She had a lot more faith in old Henreid than I did, but that's another can of worms.

BH: How would you sum up Bette Davis?

PL: Shrewd. [*taps forefinger against side of head*] Very shrewd. Lucky, too. Look at her career, at how many times she was saved after everyone had given her up for dead. She got *All About Eve*, and coasted through the fifties on it. *Baby Jane*, a very profitable piece of shit, and damn if she didn't coast right through the sixties on *that*. I'd sell my soul for a *third* of that woman's luck!

　　Or as Bette might say at this very moment in time, "Oh, Petah, Petah, Petah!" [*laughs uproariously*]

THE WOMEN

Q: I have here a copy of a filmography that includes all your movies....

A: [*beams*] Yes, that's very good for the casts and credits of my pictures.

Q: It's nicely illustrated. May I go through it and mention particular women with whom you've worked?

A: Feel free. [*lights cigarette*]

Q: You don't tire of questions about your work or co-stars?

A: Not if they're asked sincerely.

Q: Oh, they are! And I'll try not to ask the same old questions. Much of what I want to know hasn't been asked, or so it seems.

A: Ask away. But why not start at the beginning. Chronology is better for me. [*settles back into seat expectantly*]

Q: Now, then. Zasu Pitts was in your first two films, in 1931 at Universal. I'm almost embarrassed to admit, because it's become almost mandatory to make fun of her, but I always liked her a lot, and still do.

A: That kind of loyalty is good. Don't let critics or trends dissuade you. Miss Pitts did highlight several of the pictures in which she got increasingly small roles.

Q: Why are some performers, especially nonbeautiful actresses, put down so much?

A: In her case, she had a nervous habit of fluttering her hands. It became widely imitated, until it was a joke.

Q: In one movie, W. C. Fields called her dumb.

A: Fields had a wicked tongue. He once said Mae West was a plumber's idea of Cleopatra. God knows what he said about *me*! Of course, he wouldn't have dared say it in a *movie.*

Q: Loretta Young is another actress whom it's become chic to disparage, but not because she wasn't attractive. Why, then?

A: [*rolls eyes*] I think because she is so self-righteous, and young people today have little time for that sort of thing. I did not work with her; we had completely different styles. She was famous for paying more attention [*on her TV series*] to her clothes than to anything else. I left my costumes to experts like Orry-Kelly.

Q: I digress, but I've always wondered why your lipstick is drawn on well beyond your natural lip line?

A: [*tensely*] You mean you think I wear too *much*?

Q: Well…no, it suits you. It's a trademark. Like, Joan Crawford also painted her lips larger than life.

A: [*winces*] I nevah noticed....When I was on the stage, somebody said that I had very large eyes—which any idiot can
see! And he said that by comparison my lips were very
small. Well, in those days, tiny lips were the fashion. They
were thought quite feminine and desirable, and I suppose
men preferred women with smaller mouths who didn't
talk too much! [*laughs*]

But I realized that, dramatically, a larger mouth was a
must. So audiences could *see* it, for one thing.

Q: But what about movies, with close-ups?

A: It still looked good. I needed that, to compensate for my
big eyes and eyelids. Oh, I used to be terribly self-conscious
about my eyelids.

Q: I have the same.

A: Then you know that when one is complimented on what
one considers a slight defect, one feels apprehensive. I
hated it when someone would write about my "pop-eyes."
Just hated it!

Q: Loretta Young...?

A: Oh. [*a long drag of her cigarette*] Go on, if you must.

Q: You were explaining why she isn't held in high esteem in
certain quarters.

A: ...You probably heard she has always been terribly reli-
gious. Some would say devout, some would say fanatical.
She used to keep a swear-box on her sets, and anyone who
ever used a swear word was pressured by her into putting
in a nickel or twenty-five cents or whatever into this box.
The story goes that Barbara Stanwyck—I think—once
used a "damn," and Loretta—then young, like her name—
insisted that Miss Stanwyck put a quarter into her little

box. Miss Stanwyck said, "Here's five dollars, Loretta. Why don't you go *fuck* yourself?" [*cackles*]

Q: Oh, I love it!

A: Yet I find it a little difficult to believe, because I don't think Barbara ever worked with Young....

Q: She may just have been visiting the set. But you worked with Stanwyck, didn't you?

A: ...[*waiting for me to be specific*]

Q: In a movie of Edna Ferber's best-selling novel *So Big*. You had a scene together. What was it like?

A: Yes, yes, yes, I remember. It was Warners. I think it was my second year in Hollywood [*1932*]. Of course, *she* was the star, in *those* days. I was doing one of my blonde glamour-puss roles they'd saddled me with, while *she* got to act. She aged in the movie and got to play old, which was something *I* longed to do. And of course later did, often.

Q: How did she treat you?

A: [*shrugs*] I don't think we paid each other much attention.

Q: Because Lucille Ball and others have said that, when they were starting out and working with her, Ginger Rogers didn't treat them very well.

A: In reality, an established star does tend to lord it over the newcomers. I tried not to, but neither did I have time to chum around with cast and crew unnecessarily. I was there to work. Nor did I believe—unlike the ridiculous Miss Crawford—in being followed around by a retinue of servants and sycophants.

Q: What's your opinion of Young as an actress?

A: She is...competent....Do you know the story about *The*

Jezebel (1938)

In the early years, the studios were bent on making her a glamour girl. Only Katharine Hepburn and Greta Garbo refused to do cheesecake—and got away with it.

Top, publicity photo. Above, Bette Davis, Joan Blondell, and Ann Dvorak, in appropriately enough, *Three On a Match* (1932).

Sometimes it seemed as if Bette Davis was born with a cigarrette in her hand. She probably did more to promote smoking than Joe Camel.

Top left, Bette and her mother
Ruthie Favor Davis.

Below left, Davis and Leslie Howard in
Of Human Bondage (1934). Howard was icy
with Bette becouse "he knew I would steal
the show."

Top right, Miss Davis's *Dark Victory* (1939)
co-star George Brent told her, "Bette, I
envy you. You are so special, while I am so
ordinary." Brent was once described as a
"second-rate Ronald Colman."

Bottom, Miss Davis on her relationship with
Joan Crawford, seen here with Jack Warner:
"I did *not* feud with her. Hated her guts,
but we did not feud at all."

Bette Davis and husband Number Four, Gary Merrill, as they co-starred with Anne Baxter in *All About Eve* (1950).

At a cocktail party in New York in the sixties, the legend of legends Davis shares a table with the screen's "Perfect Wife" Myrna Loy (left) and Constance Bennett (right), once the highest paid star in Hollywood.

Davis' expression in this scene from *Hush, Hush, Sweet Charlotte* (1965) pretty well sums up her feelings for co-star Joan Crawford.

Mrs. Skeffington (1943)

All About Eve (1950)

The Little Foxes (1941)

Of Human Bondage (1934)

The Private Lives Of Elizabeth And Essex (1939)

Dead Ringer (1964)

TV's *Hotel* (1982)

Death on the Nile (1978)

Crusades? No? Good. Well, she was in it, and De Mille was directing, and I don't recall who the leading man was, but someone said he was homosexual, so you may want to find out [*the year was 1935, the male lead was Henry Wilcoxon; ironically, a close friend of homophobic C. B.*]. Miss Young was playing Richard the Lion-Hearted's wife, and her line was, "Richard, you've got to save Christianity!" Which, the way she said it—and people criticized *me* for enunciating!—it came out, "Richard, you gotta save Christianity!"

De Mille was having great patience with her, but he took her aside and asked her to put more awe into her line-reading. So they re-shot the scene, and she said, "Aw, Richard, you gotta save Christianity!" [*roars with laughter*]

Q: Do you know something? I'd heard that before, only it wasn't about Loretta Young, it was about John Wayne—in another Christian spectacle, in the sixties.

A: Really? Well!

Q: Maybe it's apocryphal.

A: Even so, I could see either of them doing that line-reading.

Q: Me too. And yet each one won an Oscar.

A: [*a big frown, with the lips turning way down*] *That*, over the years, has become just another popularity contest!

Q: What do you think of Stanwyck as an actress?

A: ...Crews certainly like her [*smirking*]. To them, she's "one of the boys...."

Q: She's never been a favorite of mine, but I think she's gotten better with age.

A: Yes, that can be said of most performers.

Q: Did you at any point envy her career?

A: Yes, only when she did that Western thing on television [The Big Valley]. It ran for *years*! *That* is the sort of thing *I* should have done. I was well ahead of my time in being willing to appear on television. Stars never did, at first.

Q: Noel Coward once said that TV is something you appear on, not something to watch.

A: I disagree [*taking Coward at face value*]. I knew it had a very big future, and was prepared to do a series. But it just didn't happen [*until* Hotel, *which was soon followed by major health problems for Bette Davis*].

Q: Do you find it hard to believe Loretta Young got an Oscar, yet Stanwyck didn't?

A: It was unfair, of course. Very. Another who deserved it but never got it was Rosalind Russell. Later in her career, she got to do some varied characterizations—after they finally got her out of a man's suit!

Q: Speaking of Oscar, it's said in some reference works that you named it that. True?

A: Yes, it *is* true. Some sources won't admit it.

Q: Uh, who designed the statuette?

A: Cedric Gibbons, who was art director at Metro. He was one of Hollywood's most talented homosexuals, although he was by no means one to admit it.

Q: I know—he married Dolores Del Rio, who also had another gay husband. Miss D., you were one of the first stars to publicly put in a word—a good word—for gay men. [*she nods*] So you were a pioneer in many ways....

A: I look at it this way: Without the Jews or homosexuals, there would have been no Hollywood.

Q: You mean all the Jewish founders of studios and the gay designers and actors?

A: Also the gentlemen who did the costumes, makeup, the music, some of our—*my*—best directors and writers, and as you say, many actors.

Q: Where would Bette Davis have been without Hollywood?

A: God knows!

Q: Looking through this book, your third film was directed by the gay Britisher James Whale....

A: *Waterloo Bridge.* I'm afraid the remake [*with Vivien Leigh and Robert Taylor*] is better known today. But ours was quite credible....Whale had a great touch and wonderful taste. But our film wasn't as memorable as his *Showboat,* or even his horrors, like *Frankenstein.*

Q: The female lead in *Waterloo Bridge* was Mae Clark. Wasn't she the silent star with the "bee-stung lips"?

A: No, that was Mae Marsh. Mae was somehow a very popular name around the turn of the century. Mae Clark was the one who got the grapefruit in the face from Cagney. I'm sure everyone must have confused those Mae's.

Q: The non-Western Mae's. Maybe that's why neither of them became a very big star.

A: That's likely. When you think about it, big stars cannot be confused with anybody else. If two people can be confused for each other, then neither really has what it takes for real stardom.

Q: You're like nobody else at all.

A: I thank you and I readily admit it. But it's important, too, that your name not be confused with anyone else's. If *you* became an actor, your first name would be an advantage!

Q: Misspelled, but an advantage!

A: And you can see how a gimmick like the bee-stung lips is simply not enough to sustain an entire career. As I said before, I was concerned with my lips, but I knew that was only one small part of my package. I always thought what I said and how I said it and reacted—because, really, acting is basically reacting—was more important than how I looked.

Q: Speaking of names, Bette Midler was named after you. Did you know, though, that she had two sisters and they were named after Judy Garland and Susan Hayward?

A: Her mother must have been devoted to movies!

Q: I'm sure. 'Course, people pronounce your and Midler's first names differently....

A: Well, *Bette* [*as in Midler*] *is* the correct way. Because that is what Balzac intended. But my mother thought it was pronounced the same as Betty. While Miss Midler's mother mistakenly thought *my* name was pronounced "bet." Both our mothers were wrong!

Q: But well-intentioned. And Hollywood didn't even want you to be Bette or Betty.

A: They believed in whole makeovers! [*shakes head*] The reason they wanted me renamed, so they said, was because I sounded, to *them*, English! So they strongly suggested I become Miss *Davies*.

Q: Which is a Welsh name.

A: Exactly! You *know*. Which is how stupid Hollywood could be! Then they wanted me to change both names, and one of their godawful concoctions was *Bettina Dawes*. I informed them in no uncertain terms that I would not go through life known as Between the Drawers!

Q: So, your name is really your own. Unlike Ms. Crawford, whose two names were given her from the result of a movie magazine fan contest.

A: Hmph! An artificial woman, from start to finish....But talk about her, if we must, some other time. I've just had my lunch....

Q: Well...Hedda Hopper—that great thespian—was in one of your movies....

A: Only one? Poor thing, she was in everybody's movies. Nevah had one of her own.

Q: I guess no one remembered her till she took up a pen, thereby proving the pen is mightier than the bit part.

A: A thoroughly unpleasant woman.

Q: You worked with Joan Blondell. I got to meet and interview her. She was charming.

A: Yes, a wonderful, wonderful person. No pretensions, and she was unique in that she never stabbed anyone in the back. She really was too nice for her own good. She had been a star, but she just couldn't fight the men at the top. [*shakes head ruefully*] She didn't want to fight. She felt her peace of mind was more important than her career.

Q: Unlike you.

A: Oh, I'm different from that! Constitutionally, I can stand a good fight. I relish it! I liked fighting, *and* I had my peace of mind.

Q: Is that due to intestinal fortitude, or what?

A: I think so. I've been told time and again that I have nerves of steel. I'm simply lucky.

Q: Remember the film *The Turning Point*? Shirley MacLaine had a line where she tells Anne Bancroft, and I paraphrase, "You'd walk over anybody, and still get a good night's sleep." Is that basically the attitude one needs to succeed in Hollywood?

A: [*smiles*] I'm afraid it is not a pretty business. Simply because there is so much at stake.

Q: The more I see of Hollywood, the more I realize that even the best-loved or most goody-goody stars have a second personality which their public never sees.

A: It appears only behind the scenes.

Q: Does a star have to be ruthless?

A: ...Well, there are really two ways of being ruthless. I have been ruthlessly single-minded about my work—roles, career, the *quality* of it. Even when I knew a script was crap, I did my best and expected everyone else to—because it was *my* name above the title, and the supporting cast never gets blamed, but the star always does, especially a woman star.

Q: And there's no way to avoid an occasional crappy script, right?

A: Right. When one is very young, you get a crappy script, then when you are middle-aged and beyond, it is mostly what you get offered. But the alternative is to not work, or to take years off in between quality films, and by then they've forgotten you. The public is terribly fickle. They've been good to *me*, but this has as much to do with my persistence as their loyalty.

Q: What's the second way of being ruthless?

A: Using people, betraying them. *That*, I have not done. I will sacrifice myself to my career, but I do not sacrifice my friends to it. Nor indeed anyone else, knowingly.

Q: So, ruthless dedication's all right....You worked with Mayo Methot in a few pictures. Today she's remembered solely as Bogart's first wife.

A: No, she was not his first. His first was a stage actress that I remember very clearly. Helen Mencken. She was in a notorious but successful Broadway play about lesbians. It was called *The Captive*, and in the 1920s everyone was talking about it—in whispers!

Q: I'm surprised it was allowed long enough to become a hit, what with the extreme censorship.

A: Well, if it had been about *men*, it wouldn't have been a hit. As you say, it would have been closed down. But with women…people just couldn't believe it about *women*.

Q: You mean they couldn't imagine lesbians doing anything? Together?

A: Except knitting [*smirks*].

Q: As Joan Crawford did?

A: …She did a lot of things [*dourly*].

Q: Mayo Methot was the wife with whom Bogey had the legendary fights, wasn't she?

A: The most jealous woman I ever heard tell about. Temperamental? It's a wonder she didn't kill the poor man. She used to bruise him, awfully. The Battling Bogarts, they were called. But by the time we worked together [*in 1934*], she was on the outs.

Q: As an actress, you mean? [*she nods*] So she didn't dare display her temperament on the set?

A: That's correct.

Q: We hear of older actresses often treating younger ones abominably. What about hot young actresses doing the same to fading older actresses?

A: It happens. You mean to me, of course? I thought you did.…Yes, I worked with a younger but grossly untalented actress not too long ago. Never became a star, but at that time she was co-starring in every third film made in Hollywood. When we were introduced on the set, she pretended I was her favorite relic. I put her right in her place, showed her I was not about to be her pet dowager, and she showed her true colors—didn't speak to me the rest of the shoot. Which was fortunate for me, since every third word which came out of her mouth was "fuck" or "shit."

Q: A bitchy profession you chose, Miss Davis.

A: [*smiles proudly*] But more so in the theater.

Q: Why?

A: I don't know. On the other hand, theater is kinder to an older actress. On a stage, she can play much younger than her age, if she stays slim. The *camera*, though! It is a middle-aged actress' cruelest enemy. Worse than any rival....The funny thing is, when I was coming into pictures, probably the biggest actress in Hollywood was Marie Dressler—top billing, top dollar, everything. She was on top of the popularity polls too. Now I look back at her— and her performances on screen do hold up well—I envy and admire her. Of course, at the time, I didn't give her a moment's thougpht, would never have *thought* of seeking her out for advice. Youth: *entirely* wrapped up in itself!

Q: Wasn't it Shaw who said that youth is wasted on the young?

A: Whoever said it was absolutely right.

Q: It's better for women now in Hollywood. Now, a woman is labeled over the hill at forty, maybe fifty, but in the thirties it was closer to thirty, am I right?

A: Oh, yes. And *forty* was a dirty word. Now, forty is not much at all, and everyone exercises and everyone has plastic surgery and eats right. *We* did none of that. *I* certainly didn't, and by forty-five, I did not look that wonderful, I have to admit.

Q: There was no Jane Fonda Workout then....

A: [*snickers*] If there'd been a Henry Fonda Workout, I wouldn't even have done *that*! To me, exercise is for athletes—although I have to admire the actresses who do it, and *envy* them!

Q: Getting back to your female co-stars, you worked numerous times with Olivia de Havilland. Did that improve or impede your friendship?

A: Our friendship is strong. Sometimes Olivia had a role as big as I did, sometimes she supported me. But we've remained friends, and when Crawford was pulled off of [Hush, Hush,] *Sweet Charlotte*, I specifically asked for Olivia to replace her. She did a wonderful job!

Q: In *Dark Victory*, Geraldine Fitzgerald has said, you helped her out as a newcomer.

A: [*beaming*] Well, as I always say, I put the entire picture above myself. If we *all* did well, then the picture did well, and we all advanced.

Q: But Miriam Hopkins was famed for her temperament....

A: She was a bitch. Ask anybody who worked with her, ever. I know for a fact that she never changed or mellowed, later. Always had to upstage everyone! You may have heard of *These Three*. It was a film of Lillian Hellman's play *The Children's Hour*, about lesbians. Hopkins was in the film.

So was Merle Oberon, and she said she would sooner have an abortion than have Hopkins for a co-star again!

Q: Oy! Had she had an abortion?

A: I believe that's why,—because of an illegal one,—she could never have children.

Q: It's a wonder Hopkins wasn't forcibly retired.

A: Well, she should have been! But as I was attempting to say, she was in *These Three.* Then, in the 1960s, the great director William Wyler remade it as *The Children's Hour*, because there was less censorship by then. And Hopkins was in it again, only this time in support, as an aunt. You ask Shirley MacLaine if Miss Hopkins *still* wasn't trying to interfere with blockings and scenes, and making a complete ass of herself! *Hope*less!

Q: Twice you worked with Ms. Hopkins [The Old Maid *and* Old Acquaintance].

A: Incredibly, they were good films, despite her silly antics.

Q: Would you have worked with her a third time?

A: Even I can stand only so much. She had talent, but talent without professionalism is not much. And I do not possess a streak of masochism. Not by a *long* shot!

Q: In *The Great Lie*, critics said you virtually handed Mary Astor her Academy Award on a platter.

A: I was good in it, and she was good in it. [*shrugs*] What's wrong with that? I already had two Oscars, and Mary finally got one, and I was delighted. She earned it.

Q: When I saw it on TV, I was surprised that you played the good woman rather than the bad one.

A: *That* is why Mary got the award. She played against type, and so did I. Of course, audiences loved me, so long as I was in a good story. I shuttled between good and evil, and people accepted this because I was known as versatile. I did *not* want to be trapped in a pigeonhole. But critics saw me only as bad women, and I think this is where my supposedly bitchy reputation got started. A bitch is more memorable than a sweet housewife. And anyway, the media always wants to put a tag on you—just as they always saw poor Ingrid Bergman as *good.*

Q: Which proved her undoing, when that image conflicted with an ordinary woman's private life.

A: It shows you how dangerous stereotypes can be. They can even limit you in your private life....But the worst has got to be a sex symbol, so-called. *Those* women were severely limited in their roles, like Rita Hayworth or Marilyn [*Monroe*], and the men in their lives expected 1001 Arabian Nights. The *fools!*

Q: Hayworth even said that, when a man married her, he went to bed with *Gilda,* but woke up with Rita.

A: ...I feel sorry for her, very sorry. If a career is based on beauty, then it can't amount to much.

Q: Not over the long haul. Did you deliberately choose sympathetic roles, as in *The Great Lie,* to balance your villainesses?

A: No, no, I didn't do good-bad-good-bad. How mechanical! I opted for the best role available at the time—I always have. But in *The Great Lie,* there were two good roles, and I felt like playing the role which I did. I'd had my choice of either one, of course. And I knew full well that the actress playing the "bad" one would steal the show. I campaigned for Mary to play her—she was a friend of mine.

When I starred in *Charlotte*, I asked them to give Mary a role. It was small, but crucial, and she was grateful. She was a few years older than me, but by the time we did *Charlotte*, she looked *ages* older. It was her last [*film*].

Q: Could you, at that time, have played nothing but villainesses and survived?

A: ...Not really. If audiences never saw you as anything but evil, they would come to hate you. They were much more literal then.

Q: Another actress who was great at being bad, albeit in supporting roles, was Gale Sondergaard.

A: A fine actress and a fine human being. The first to win a supporting actress Oscar [*in 1936*]. I helped campaign for them to add a supporting category, and as you must know, I was a president of the Academy—the first woman president....

Q: A well-known fact [*she smiles, with a slight nod or bow of her head*]. Ms. Sondergaard is most famous as the villainess in *The Letter*, one of my favorite films.

A: She was excellent. Though, technically, *I* was the villain—as the story eventually revealed. Gale played the awful Eurasian. She was Scandinavian but looked so exotic. Later, she was also in *Juarez* with me.

Q: Tragically, the Hollywood political witch hunts destroyed her career.

A: Yes, it was very sad. Many good people lost their livelihoods. Some killed themselves.

Q: Yet today, Reagan denies the witch hunts even occurred, or that there were blacklists....

A: He's either a liar or has a terrible memory. I'd rather imagine he has a bad memory.

Q: For years, you weren't invited to the Reagan White House.

A: Neither was every other actor or actress.

Q: However, you were on good terms with Presidents Kennedy and Carter?

A: [*nods*] They were not only good leaders, but lovely men. They happened to be fans of mine.

Q: Back to the women. *Now, Voyager* is arguably your most popular movie. One can't watch Dame Gladys Cooper in it as your mother without hissing her.

A: You wish to know if she was a bitch or a goody-two-shoes? [*smiles*] Neither. She was nice, but reserved. English, of course. Didn't deliver a Boston accent. But the one I didn't especially care for, who was bitchy in the film and off, was Bonita Granville.

Q: Oh, that child actress.

A: She was no child in *Now, Voyager.*

Q: A teen, I guess. She was best known for *Hitler's Children.* I believe she passed away recently. What was wrong with your relationship?

A: Nothing was wrong with *my* relationship! *She's* the one who carried on. I don't remember any details I care to bring up, but she struck me as flighty and gossipy.

Q: Oh. Now, Thelma Ritter [*of* All About Eve]. She must be almost everybody's favorite character actress. What was she really like? Just like on screen, one hopes?

A: ...In life, as in pictures. Thelma Ritter—nobody played a better servant.

Q: Or more regally. She helped make the opening scenes in *All About Eve* indelible. Wonderful lines she got to perform— she didn't even need lines, she had such body language.

A: Are you related to her?

Q: My great-aunt....No, I'm just kidding.

A: Well...yes, she was a real asset to *Eve*.

Q: But after the opening scenes, she suddenly disappears, and is never seen again or referred to.

A: Well, it was a long picture, and a complicated one. As a film goes along, it has to draw you into the story, and it gains momentum by focusing on the main characters. Because, really, their story and conflicts are the plot.

Q: Oh, I suppose. I mean, yeah, that's true. Um, I see in this book that one of your later films, *Another Man's Poison*, was produced by Fairbanks, Jr. Did he ever mention or talk about his first wife, our Miss Crawford?

A: [*slow frown*] No...he had long since exorcised her.

Q: Okay...*Storm Center*, in 1956, was about book-banning, which the witch hunters encouraged, then as now. You weren't the originally cast star, were you?

A: Mary Pickford. As an initially meek librarian who defends keeping a controversial book on the shelves. So that it can be judged or condemned on its own merits and not by hearsay.

Q: That was a brave topic, for the fifties.

A: Yes, highly controversial. And it did *not* receive a very wide distribution, which was no accident....

Q: Alas, it wasn't a hit.

A: No, it wasn't, but it became very admired by a lot of people. But [*shrugs*] it doesn't pay to be ahead of one's time—you have to wait a long time for your pat on the back! [*smiles*]

Q: Did the controversy scare Pickford out of the role?

A: I think so. That, and vanity. It would have been her big comeback. Like Garbo, she was always rumored to be on the verge of a major comeback. She hadn't done anything in even longer than Garbo, and I'm sure that after playing so many little girls, she had second thoughts about the camera. I mean, she was there when they invented the original close-up!

Q: It's probably as well you did *Storm Center*. I can't see her bringing much weight to that role.

A: I accepted the part in an instant. I nevah let my vanity interfere with my taking up a role which somebody else was offered first. Their loss was my gain!

Q: Did you ever stop to think whether being in *Storm Center* might have harmed your career? After all, the blacklists weren't officially over till the sixties.

A: Well, I didn't take that into consideration. [*pause*] Much.

Q: Was it a big comedown, playing Debbie Reynolds's mother in *The Catered Affair* [1956]?

A: [*smirking*] I'm not sure how you mean that! But Gore Vidal did a fine script, and by then I looked very much like a matronly mother, so I played one. Unlike anyone I'd played—a very working-class, untalkative woman. Of course, I looked *awful,* and the comedown was seeing myself magnified horribly on the screen, but I later lost the weight.

Q: Your role required some pretty dismal clothes and hair.

A: Oh, I know! But then, to boost my spirits and my image, I turned around and played Catherine the Great in an epic [*John Paul Jones*]. I looked wonderful in *that*.

Q: Yet far more people saw *The Catered Affair*....

A: Mmm. It was a better film, no question. And my role was bigger.

Q: Soon after that, you played Ann-Margret's mother, in Frank Capra's last movie, *A Pocketful of Miracles*.

A: Oh, let's not go over whose mothers I played! *Please*. By a certain age, an actress is automatically going to play *someone's* mother, and I would have played the mother of Frankenstein, if it was a good part! *That's* what mattered.

Q: You said an actor picks the best of what's offered, but the pickings must have been richer in the thirties and forties, yes?

A: That is *so* right. *Oh*, yes. In the late 1930s, early 1940s— really the golden age for film—I had to turn down *wonderful* parts. I just couldn't play everything offered me! But later [*shakes head slowly*], I had to pick the best of a very indifferent lot of stories.

Q: Why, after World War II, did women's roles decline so much in quantity and quality?

A: I think it was a backlash. During the war, women had done men's jobs. After, Hollywood must have thought the best way to get women back in their traditional place was by going back a few decades on the screen. Careers were out, home was in.

Q: What about, also, the 1950s, when the Democrats were finally out of the White House for the first time since 1932?

A: The witch hunts. Yes. Well, I'm sure that in part they were a reaction to Roosevelt; and they had an *awful* impact on scripts. Serious issues were suspect, and strong women were suspect, *every*thing was suspect.

Q: So, the actresses being created were airheads—

A: Their roles, as well.

Q: It was the time of the passive blonde [*she sighs*]. People like Marilyn, Jayne, Debbie, June, Doris, Sandra, etc.

A: [*a disgusted frown*] Set us back twenty, thirty years!

Q: The pendulum swings. In the sixties, women were back, but ever since, there's been a scriptwriter's backlash against the women's rights movement.

A: The problem could be solved overnight *if…*half the script-writers were women.

Q: …I've always thought it must be real fun to play with your-self as a co-star. I mean, to be twins [*as in* A Stolen Life, *1946, and* Dead Ringer, *1964*]. I'll bet that secretly every actor would love to co-star with himself or herself?

A: It *is* balm for your ego! No need to battle your co-star, that's true. But my, it is hard work, it really is! In *Dead Ringer*, I had to murder myself, and then one twin dis-robes the corpse and puts on her clothes. We had to exe-cute that scene—no pun intended—like clockwork. They had to nail the furniture to the floor so that it hadn't moved an inch when we reshot it with me playing the *other* one.

Q: In Spanish, "the other one" is *La Otra*, which was the title of the Dolores Del Rio film of which *Dead Ringer* was an

English-language remake. Did you know that, Miss Davis?

A: That Del Rio had done it? No, Boze, I did not. Wait—I think somebody may have told me, once.

Q: In this book, there's a surprising still from the movie of Harold Robbins's *Where Love Has Gone*. Susan Hayward's in a long gown, you're there—dressed as a rich matron— and Joey Heatherton, though very young [*as Davis's grand-daughter*], doesn't have as good legs as you do!

A: You think so? [*smiles, but doesn't move to see the photo*] Well, in real life, a few men have had the courage to compliment my legs. No critic ever did, because I wasn't known for that. Men seem to think I won't appreciate a nice compliment about my looks. I *do*! As long as they don't dwell on it too much. Unlike Grable or Dietrich, my legs were not more famous than my talent....

Q: I'm sure they envied you when Oscar time rolled around.

A: *I* never envied another actor, ever. Private life, that's another matter.

Q: In the seventies, at the drive-in, I saw *Burnt Offerings*, with Karen Black and Oliver Reed. [*she groans*] I was disappointed how small your role was, though you received prominent billing.

A: [*a pained pause*] That billing was no kindness. I fought for it, and they'd probably have given it to me in any case because it was a self-styled horror film, and the producer thought my name drew patrons to that type of film [*shakes head*].

Q: Was it a bad experience, making it?

A: ...The actress [*pronounced as two separate words*] who tried to treat me as an old relic, then wouldn't speak to me off-camera is the one you have just mentioned. *Next* question....

Q: Did people often ask why you took smaller roles or roles in mediocre movies like *Burnt Offerings*?

A: [*exhales a large puff of smoke*] They asked. And sometimes I had to point out the *obvious*—which is, sometimes you have to make a living! Especially if you're a mother!

Q: At the end of the seventies you won an Emmy for *Strangers: The Story of a Mother and Daughter*.

A: Yes, that was a good part, and a big one. Two people, really. But I've never declined a role just because it's small.

Q: Still, I bet you prefer bigger roles.

A: [*smiling*] I am a ham, at heart.

Q: In *Strangers*, you had a very strained relationship with your daughter Gena Rowlands. Many actors would maintain an aloofness with the fellow actor so that it parallels the plot's relationship. How about you?

A: That is *Method* acting. I can be friendly with somebody, then curse her in a scene, one minute later. However, I do not believe a set is the place for socializing. When I'm there, I'm there to work.

Q: I've been told by some actors who've worked with you that you set the pace for the rest of the cast on the set.

A: Yes, it is up to the star. Everyone follows her lead. If she is causing unpleasantness or acting irresponsibly, then it will not be a happy set or an efficient one. Unfortunately, being on time is less strictly observed than it used to be. But I've been lucky with *most* of the younger actors I've worked with. *Most* are professionals.

Q: Unlike Faye Dunaway? [*Davis sharply criticized Dunaway's tardiness on* The Tonight Show *and elsewhere.*]

A: *God!* I've said enough about *her.* [*They co-starred as daughter and mother in a telefilm about Aimee Semple McPherson, whom Davis had wanted to portray in her youth.*]

Q: Wouldn't work with her again under any circumstances? Even for a really good role?

A: [*shakes head firmly*] If my role were good, *hers* would be bigger, simply because she happens to be a younger actress—if I may use that word in connection with *her.*

Q: You co-starred with an all-star cast in *Death on the Nile,* a follow-up to the hit *Murder on the Orient Express.*

A: It was *not* a sequel. I'm glad you didn't use that foul word. It was very good, and had nothing to do with the other film—even the actor who played the detective [*Poirot*] was different.

Q: I enjoyed it immensely, saw it three times. Speaking of three, Ingrid Bergman won her third Oscar [*this time as supporting actress*] in *Orient Express,* and Lauren Bacall was nominated too. Did you have any hope of a third Oscar via *Death on the Nile?*

A: Hah! *Not* once I saw how small and one-dimensional my role was! I played a pearl thief, and Maggie Smith was my maid—or more like a female butler. They cut our scenes, our marvelous wrangling scenes, and it was a *terrible* time, doing that film on location. Just too many people in it.

Q: You and Angela Lansbury were the ones who stood out.

A: Well, she played a drunk, so right away she had an advantage. Drunks get laughs, guaranteed. I didn't choose that route. *My* part had dignity.

Q: Ms. Lansbury's been lucky in her later years to become a TV star. Yet I like her best in movies and on stage.

A: Oh, she's been *very* lucky.

Q: Are you friends?

A: ...Yes, we are.

Q: How was the great Agnes Moorehead to work with?

A: She was my maid in *Sweet Charlotte*. A great character actress, of course. You'll probably mention she was on that [*TV*] series *Bewitched*, but that was a waste of her time. She even told me she did it just for the money. Which *I* would have done *too*. But she was much better in motion pictures.

Q: Would you, though, have taken as token a role as the mother-in-law on *Bewitched*?

A: Hopefully not. Not unless the money was phenomenal and the billing above the title. I did many television pilots. Of course, none of them went over, but I played judges and other important figures. I would nevah have consented to play somebody's granny sitting in a chair in the background!

Q: Good for you. You know, Moorehead is another one who never got an Oscar.

A: A pity. Really. She was very professional, indeed. I liked her, and she liked me. She was quite relieved when Miss Crawford left our set for good!

Q: We haven't much touched on Ms. Crawford yet....

A: Hah! I won't touch that line....

Q: A professional, no doubt?

A: She was professional. I, of course, was—am—professional. We did our jobs [*on* Baby Jane]. That's it. We *had* to be pro's—the shooting schedule was just like television, it was so fast!

Q: So, no feud to report?

A: Not on the set, no. [*winks*] But if we ever talk about *behind* the scenes....

Q: You mean some of your legendary battles?

A: [*smiles, nodding energetically*]

Q: You were once quoted as saying that the best time you ever had on a movie set was in *Baby Jane,* when you kicked Joan Crawford down the stairs. [*she laughs*] But there's no such scene in the movie. Not in the final version, anyway.

A: I was speaking figuratively. But...[*irritably*] Oh, save her for another time. Why ruin a good mood?

Q: Yet we're talking about your co-stars and leading ladies....

A: *Miss* Crawford...was *no* lady! Now, I am tired, so let's call it a day [*begins to rise*].

Q: At least [*mumbled aside*].

HER CO-STAR: AGNES MOOREHEAD

*L*ate 1973. Cake and coffee at the Santa Barbara Biltmore's Coral Casino. With Agnes Moorehead, the *grande dame* of supporting actresses, whom I've interviewed earlier in the year at her Beverly Hills home. Moorehead, who loves Santa Barbara, is in town for pleasure; we meet again on condition that this time we not discuss her private life. The week before, I've been riveted by *Hush, Hush, Sweet Charlotte* and its Southern-Gothic performances by Davis and Moorehead, as her protective but doomed maid, Velma.

The two actresses are not close friends, but mutual admirers of each other's work. "Bette admires some of my roles, and I admire several of hers."

BH: You don't seem like you'd be intimidated, no matter who you were working with....

AM: I'll take that as a compliment. If you're referring to Miss Davis, you should know that her bark is worse than her bite. She is no less and no more exacting than I am, but she has been called difficult far more often.

BH: Because her roles are larger, do you think?

AM: There is no such thing as an Agnes Moorehead picture. My roles take a few weeks, less than that. I'm not around long enough to give anyone a headache! [*laughs softly*]

BH: And not having to carry an entire film, you don't get the blame if it isn't a hit.

AM: I have the best of both worlds, because I have worked just as often as I've wanted to.

BH: The natural aging process must be far harder on a female star than a character actress?

AM: [*slightly defensive*] It's hard on everyone, and not just actresses. Even John Wayne isn't doing the things he used to do, nor as often.

BH: But character actors and actresses don't usually play, in fact never play, romantic leads....

AM: Bette Davis is not a vain woman. Not as much as most actresses. One thing I always admired was her willingness to look however a characterization required. Now, in *Charlotte* she didn't look as extreme as in *Whatever Happened to Baby Jane?*, but she did look bad in many scenes.

BH: You too did a visual change of pace. Your housekeeper role had no glamour at all.

AM: No glamour! My goodness, the creature was as homely as a mud fence, apart from acting like she's touched in the head! But I was in good company, with Bette. I was quite comfortable, regardless.

BH: Joan Crawford was originally in *Charlotte*. What happened?

AM: She became ill, or claimed she did, and when her doctor supplied Mr. Aldrich [*director-producer*] with a medical certificate, the set shut down. Then the powers that be— among them, Miss Davis—decided to carry on without Miss Crawford.

BH: How did Crawford react to Davis, as a co-star and a woman?

AM: That's difficult to say, not being in on all that. The two women rubbed each other the wrong way, that's all. They had nothing in common, and I am certain that although both resented the other, Joan had a greater animosity.

BH: Why?

AM: I think because Bette is more gifted, and people think of her as a great actress, despite her increasing tendency to overact.

BH: Davis made a public statement that she was an actress, while Crawford was a movie star, and I read that Crawford took great offense.

AM: That's their difference in image. Joan is remembered for her clothes and her fashion trend-setting, with the shoulder pads and ankle-strap shoes....She worked at MGM, which meant glamour, while Warners, where Bette worked, was more closely associated with realism and some excellent social-problem films. MGM was bigger, but today the critics esteem Warners highly.

BH: Plus, Davis keeps on working, while Crawford is apparently retired.

AM: Bette works and she receives awards. I doubt Joan has received any awards in quite some time.

BH: There have been persistent rumors [*some since recorded in print*] about Bette Davis's sexuality, which has been in doubt in some quarters because of her very strong image.

AM: It is more unusual to find that many rumors about an *actress*. But Bette Davis has a very…I'm searching for a feminine word which is the equivalent of "macho."

BH: Macha?

AM: [*smiles mischievously, like Endora on* Bewitched] Something in that vein. Because of that, there have been rumors about Bette since I don't know when. She's not as vulnerable or feminine as she was during the first several years [*in Hollywood*]. That's just aging—actresses, like most women, do tend to get a little harder with age. Or even a bit—

BH: Masculine?

AM: No. Androgynous. Look at Lucille Ball. I worked with her on *The Big Street*; she was so beautiful and quite feminine. A little less so on *Lucy*, and less so now.

BH: I heard that Elizabeth Taylor once asked Bette, in the powder room, about the rumor that she and Mary Astor had been lovers. Did you ever hear that?

AM: [*nods slightly*] Bette replied that she'd had *four* husbands, in the version I heard.

BH: As did Crawford. Who was bisexual.

AM: Let's wind this up with your question about how Joan treated Bette. Bette isn't one to hold a grudge; Joan is— don't ask me how I know, but I do. But Bette did resent the way Joan would try and present herself as far more feminine, not to mention fashionable, than Bette. Bette is an innately feminine woman who is secure enough not to keep making a show of herself in jewels and furs and upswept hair. But Joan Crawford makes a practice of looking and acting that way, and I'm sure it finally got on Bette's nerves.

BH: What do you think is the secret of Bette Davis's lasting stardom?

AM: She looks *forward.* She looks forward to each new role, and she has never gotten stuck in some past decade, trying to recreate a look or role she particularly liked. She knows when it's time to move on. Variety is the spice of her life.

BH: You're right. There are some older actresses who haven't changed their hairstyle in thirty or forty years, and Miss Davis looks different every few years.

AM: Older actresses sometimes like to repeat a certain role. But Bette told me that she never liked playing younger than herself. She's not ashamed of being middle-aged, and she'd rather play her own age, any day. Or even older.

BEHIND THE SCENES

Q: Is it true that you once said of Marilyn Monroe, "There goes a good time that was had by all"?

A: [*emphatically*] No! I said that about someone else, a starlet. A starlet who shall remain nameless because I have forgotten her name.

Q: It's been said that you brought more people into the cinemas than all the sex symbols put together.

A: Well, I did.

Q: Were the fifties a sort of cinematic hell for you, what with the dominance of Monroe and such?

A: *Not* a good time, but Miss Monroe was not the most successful actress of that decade. I believe it was Audrey Hepburn. Two extremes of sex—one voluptuous and one almost sexless.

Q: But strong women no longer got good roles?

A: They were few and far between. I got a few good ones, and Joan did too, while Stanwyck made any old picture just to keep working. The one who really lucked out was Rosalind Russell. She was a very different type from me, but she got *Auntie Mame* and also *Picnic* and a few others. But it was a lean time, yes.

Q: Crawford got more publicity than ever by working less and marrying the head of Pepsi-Cola.

A: Hah! Something I *nevah* had to do was try and make a place for myself through some man!

Q: Why do you think in the final years she was such a recluse?

A: I think she hated losing her looks.

Q: She looked so good for so long....

A: She had at least two face-lifts. She was having plastic surgery before I knew what it meant. People were forever after me to have some, but I held out.

Q: People say that Crawford was in awe of you, professionally.

A: Hmm....

Q: You know, Miss Davis, a friend of mine hosts a local TV show called *Dialing for Dollars*, an afternoon movie show. One day, he was showing a Crawford movie and said that someone had written to ask his opinion of Crawford [*Davis leans closer*]. He said he didn't especially care for her, that he thought she was something of an ice cube, and that viewers didn't need bother to write in and criticize him, since he was entitled to his opinion.

A: Well, first of all, your friend *is* entitled to his opinion! But second, Miss Crawford continues to have loyal fans, posthumously. These are women who grew up with her. I think they identified with her clothes and furs, I don't know.

Q: She used often to play rags-to-riches heroines.

A: She was a specialist in masochism. On screen, she loved to suffer [*scornfully*].

Q: Suffering in mink, of course. Makes a difference.

A: Offscreen, I do not know if she enjoyed suffering, or only inflicting suffering. But she made certain people in the audience rooted for her. She convinced them she was what they saw—the put-upon heroine [*punctuating her words with drags of her cigarette*]. She was good at what she did, at what she settled for.

Q: You obviously don't think much of her movies.

A: Some were good, I didn't say that. I *do* think she was quite one- or two-dimensional.

Q: Could she have developed her talent further, with more challenging roles?

A: I think if she could have, she would have. Once she hit forty or so.

Q: She's one of those striving-to-be-a-lady actresses who seemed terrified of not coming across sympathetic.

A: Well, we were opposites. Both very popular, although I lasted longer. But where she built her career by playing sappy heroines, I built it by playing a variety of people: most notably, bitches. She never played a bitch because—

Q: Because she was one?

A: [*nods*]

Q: She did play bitches later on.

A: Well, age forces that on you. Eventually, we all play bitches, or we don't work, or we work once every quarter-century like Miss [*Claudette*] Colbert.

Q: I do agree with my friend that Crawford gives an impression of coldness or at least insincerity. So often, her cinematic emotions seem forced. Like in *Humoresque*. Did you see that one?

A: [*nods*] One of the most spectacular close-ups in film. She did have wonderful cheekbones [*grudgingly*]. And a good mouth—she copied my generous lipline and then my natural eyebrows, but with her, she went overboard on everything. Those eyebrows wound up looking like African caterpillars! [*guffaws*]

Q: She did innovate the shoulder pads, didn't she?

A: No, that was Adrian, the designer [*at MGM*].

Q: She sure had different phases and looks in her long career.

A: Ah! That is the difference between us: She kept seeking and going from one look to another every decade or so, but I simply was myself, and I looked the way a particular characterization required me to look.

Q: It's been said you are an actor, where she was a star. Right?

A: *That* is it.

Q: Don't you find that as a big star gets older, he or she tends to keep playing herself?

A: It's like shorthand, and sometimes the audience does not want you to stray too far from your star persona. This is why the great leading men are so predictable. Women are lucky to be allowed more emotional range.

Q: One of your imitators says in his act—to illustrate this

point—as you, "I should now like to do a scene for you from all of my films...."

A: [*stiffly, after a rather stunned pause*] I suppose that is wit. But it means very little.

Q: You don't think it has any validity.

A: Not if it's at my expense....You can look at Katharine Hepburn, whose roles never vary; she has become a *parody* of herself. You can hardly find much similarity between my roles or performances in *Jane* and *The Nanny* and *Bunny O'Hare* and...and *Burnt Offerings* or *Death on the Nile*, and on and on. *Do* you?

Q: No, you're right.

A: Well, it's much too easy for someone who's never met me and makes his living off me to generalize—and *erroneously*! [*a stung pause*] Who is he? What's his name?

Q: I don't know. I heard about whoever it was from someone else [*in reality, it was Charles Pierce*]. Now, I'm not talking about you, but about big stars as a rule. Do you agree with this—

A: [*suddenly laughing, the angry fire gone out of her eyes*] God, you're persistent! And brave.

Q: And you have a sense of humor.

A: Well, I don't know what I'd do without it [*shakes head*]. I'd otherwise have *melted*, years ago....

Q: *Wizard of Oz*, right? [*she nods*] Someone said or wrote that the typical Hollywood actress, when she starts out, tells reporters that she is interested in exploring character, and so she plays one varying role after another. But once she's a star, those circles of experimentation have become smaller, or stop. And she tells reporters that she's still interested in exploring character—her own. Though she doesn't say so....

A: [*smiles knowingly*] Yes....Yes, we are all guilty of that, to some degree. Males more so than females, as I have said, and as should be pointed out. As an old man, John Wayne always played John Wayne, but for an older actress, there is a *world* of difference between a hatchet-murderess and a doting grandmother.

Q: True. But you know what I find interesting? My friend the TV host felt compelled, having mentioned Crawford's name, to bring up yours.

A: Why is that? We're so *different*.

Q: [*carefully*] Maybe one reason is you both played so many bitchy parts. But as he said, with you, some humor always showed through. With her, the anger seemed unrelieved.

A: ...She had a much more difficult childhood than I did. By comparison, mine was a piece of cake.

Q: You had a loving mother; hers wasn't.

A: That is the most crucial influence one can have—a loving and caring mother. To make one feel one is worthwhile. I know men hate to hear it, but the father's influence is usually rather incidental.

Q: Even if he sticks around?

A: Then, it depends on the man. But he can nevah rival the mother as an influence.

Q: You and Joan both grew up without fathers....

A: I know....Did she have a sister or brother?

Q: A parasitic brother who wound up working at a motel, was

an alcoholic, and when he died, she didn't attend his funeral, though I'm pretty sure it was in L.A. To her credit, she had gotten him a studio job at MGM, long before, but he couldn't hold it.

A: Families are a very difficult thing. But who could grow up without them? It's once one becomes peers that the real problems begin.

Q: Do you care to elaborate?

A: No. Families are also a private thing.

Q: ...I have a quote here from Mirabeau, an eighteenth-century Frenchman. See if you agree. "Modesty has its falseness and the kiss its innocence."

A: [*long pause*] I agree. No use having false modesty. Even on a good actress, it comes across phony as hell. It reminds me—I knew a woman who was married to a producer. Not a good one. She bragged about him whenever she could. It was awful! You loathed bumping into her at parties. One night, she told me, "My husband is so modest." I very nearly told her, "He has a lot to be modest about."

Q: If you'd been in a movie, you would have!

A: That's why movies are often better than life.

Q: What about the second half of Mirabeau's quote, that the kiss has its innocence?

A: It *does*. Look at movie love scenes. Most are perfectly inno-cent—two professionals going through the motions. It is the audience that supplies the spice.

Q: [When you] nicknamed the Academy Award statuette "Oscar"...it had something to do with your first husband or—?

A: [*laughs*] When I saw the award's rear end, it reminded me of my husband's. Both flat.

Q: You weren't president of the Academy for long, were you?

A: Not long enough. They wanted a mere figurehead, someone famous to publicize the Academy. I didn't know that. I wanted to rule.

Q: I could see you in politics.

A: I can too!

Q: Well, if Ronald Reagan could do it....

A: And if I lived in England. Unfortunately, America is very far from giving any woman national top-billing.

Q: Why?

A: God alone knows. [*pause*] Ask *Her.*

Q: Can we get behind the scenes a little here? About feuds and good stuff like that?

A: Good stuff, yes. Juicy is fun. But I nevah had a feud. Many people I couldn't abide, but no feuds.

Q: Who, for example, couldn't you abide?

A: You really want to know?

Q: The *world* wants to know....

A: Well, *you'll* have to ask the questions, but I'll name one...Glenn Ford. Stardom went to his head. Did not know how to handle it, and he needlessly alienated people and cut short his career.

Q: How?

A: First of all, *I* gave him his first big break. I produced a picture, *A Stolen Life*, where I played twins. Old formula—a good twin and a bad twin. Later, when I played twins again, both were bad, which tells you something about our times. But anyway, *Stolen Life* was a hit, and I'd chosen Ford as my male lead, and he was able to go on to more hits.

Q: He was the lead in *Pocketful of Miracles* [*1961*]....

A: [*sourly*] *That* is part two of this little story. I agreed to do a featured role. For Mr. Capra. But Mr. Ford told the press that he had gotten me the part—which he did *not*—because he thought I could use the break! The bastard. I didn't expect him to continue being grateful for *A Stolen Life*, but neither did I expect an ego so inflated that he needed to make a false statement just to build himself up.

And he was very difficult to work with—ask anyone who has worked with him—and now he's been out of the running for a very, very long time!

Q: Some stars can't adjust to smaller roles, as you did.

A: I didn't have to adjust. I was always willing to do something good or even just for the fun of it. I once chose to do a cameo role in someone else's film, but the powers that be removed me from it because they felt I was too valuable to waste! Which shows *they* had no sense of humor. I'd play a servant, if the role was good. I *did*—in *The Nanny*.

Q: But that was a lead role.

A: A lead role, a title role and a *quality* role!

Q: Is it true that when you were new to Hollywood, Universal or Warners considered turning you into a second Jean Harlow?

A: Good heavens, *no*! If I'd heard that, I'd have left town. I had *no* desire to copy anyone, let alone such a—what was the word they invented for her?

Q: Bombshell?

A: Yes. No—"sex bomb." [*laughs*] I remember when she was initially billed as a "platinum bombshell," the studio had to explain to the public that it had nothing to do with the military. Everyone thought a platinum bombshell was a weapon!

Q: And in a way, she was.

A: [*mock-sternly, pointing a finger*] Don't be witty.

Q: I'll try and restrain myself.

A: When I hear Jean's name, I think of my poor hair. All that dyeing! Thank God I didn't lose it, the way some actresses did who went bald and had to wear wigs the rest of their lives.

Q: Who?

A: Didn't you know about Ida Lupino? I knew, because she was at Warners. Things were not as foolproof as they are now....Even Lana Turner lost her eyebrows. *I* never lost anything. Except my temper!

Q: Did you throw tantrums?

A: Of course not! What *is* a tantrum? It's something a child does, and I think you have to be on the floor to do it.

Q: Switching tracks a bit...

A: I'm *glad* you're not one-track. Feel free—but not too free!

Q: Didn't one of your servants work for Marlene Dietrich before she worked for you?

A: [*suspicious*]...She was not a servant. You mean Violla Rubber. She worked for me [*as a manager*] after she'd worked for Dietrich and I believe Diana Barrymore. When she was naughty, I would call her Shrieking Violla [*smirks*].

Q: I'll bet she told you some great stories about Dietrich?

A: Mmm-hmm. *Not* for publication...

Q: Why are some stars better known than others for having slept with almost everyone attractive in Hollywood?

A: Because it may be true. Where there's smoke...Or, they were not as discreet as they could have been. To do things like that, you had to get out of Hollywood, unless you wanted everyone to know. It was and is a small town—in *so* many ways—and the studios and columnists had spies everywhere. Including people who worked at motels.

Q: Is it true there was sort of a continental double standard, where the European actors and actresses could get away with more affairs than their American counterparts?

A: I have no doubt that was generally true. Europeans—well, they don't shock anyone, do they? But when the girl-next-door or the all-American hero fornicates, people can't believe it. If you have an accent, they *expect* you to be perverted!

Q: You've co-starred with very few top actresses. You and Dietrich or you and Hepburn would have been dynamite on the screen, don't you think?

A: With a good script.

Q: The proof is that you and Crawford had great chemistry and made cinematic history. There's a whole cult around your pairing off.

A: [*eyes bugging*] *That* is asinine. We did *one* picture, and *ever* since, I have had to endure having my name linked to hers. I could *almost* wish it had flopped!

Q: In truth, you did *two* together...[*she blinks hard*] *Hollywood Canteen*, 1944. Am I wrong?

A: You know you are not wrong. Yes, I was the founder of the real-life Hollywood Canteen, and John Garfield was the vice-president. But I did not share any scenes with darling Miss Crawford.

Q: She really had a love-hate relationship with you....Yours with her was apparently more one-track.

A: [*ignoring the second comment*] I'm not sure what you mean by love-hate.

Q: Her crush on you....

A: She got a crush on *everyone*. She even said so publicly about Garbo. She was a *fan* at heart. [*shakes head pityingly, then lights umpteenth cigarette*] No, I cannot accept the word "love" from her. She bad-mouthed me, although I'm sure she did that to everyone too.

Q: It just occurred to me that *Mildred Pierce*, which won her an Oscar, was turned down by you. Why?

A: ...Not because I would have played a mother. Or because that character was an idiot—if I'd had such a spoiled-rotten daughter, I'd have whacked her but good, I wouldn't have continued indulging her every whim! You see, if I'd done *Mildred Pierce*, the critics would all have said, "She's taking a breather." It simply was not up to my standards. A showy, very central role, yes. But no one would have given *me* an Oscar for *that*.

Q: Crawford's Oscar may partly have derived from her achieving a big comeback, don't you think?

A: Yes, after she was kicked out of Metro.

Q: When you first came to town, she was a top star.

A: Very lucky, she was. Unlike me, she was able to build all those social contacts and then make use of them. *I* had to do it the *hard* way! [*pause*] Fortunately, the hard way is usually the more lasting way.

Q: Do you think, as rumored, she slept with producers to get parts?

A: *Their* parts, you mean? [*grins*] Yes, I don't doubt it. In the beginning, that is. But *that* never got anyone any really good roles. The casting couch is strictly aid for the untalented—for small parts that don't add up to a career. Where Joan really lucked out was her choice of boyfriends. She was an incorrigible flirt, and of course the married men she carried on with wouldn't acknowledge her in public. They didn't let on, but they did give her assistance where it counted.

Then she befriended an MGM director, Eddie [*Edmund*] Goulding. He was one of *mine*, eventually—directors, I mean. He was married, and I don't know if Joan thought to have an affair with Goulding to further herself—this was in the mid-1920s or so, and everyone in Hollywood knows all this. I am not revealing anything new. But Goulding was gay, so poor promiscuous Joan came up against a dead end in that department. No pun intended.

Q: He could have been bisexual....

A: Could have been, but wasn't. We had long chats, years later. He married strictly for show. He told me how Joan had wiggled herself into his good graces, trying to vamp him. But he didn't mind, he reacted in a friendly way, and indeed they became very good chums. He was willing and very able to boost her career in various pictures. Why, I don't know.

Q: Also in that decade, wasn't Crawford very close to Billy Haines, the star whose career later ended when he was caught at the Y with a man in his cot?

A: [*nods*] He was a big star in silents. Talk around town was that Joan *proposed* to him! [*laughs*]

Q: A majority of gay actors have wed, for one reason or another, right?

A: Yes, but in those days, the way they arranged it was, they paired a gay actor with a gay actress. So that *each* had a motive to continue the marriage.

Q: Haines must have turned Crawford down.

A: You know why? No, *I* don't know. I wondered if you did. Hah! Perhaps she wasn't man enough for him.

Q: Her gay connections helped boost her up the ladder of success. No doubt her heterosexual ones did too?

A: I'm sure—wrong by wrong. You know: *ladder*…Of course, this is off the record. Just because the witch is dead, it would be terrible if such a quote got out and I was asked about it in an interview. I'd have to deny having said it.

Q: Why are stars so overly cautious about what they say about each other? As a rule.

A: I, for one, am not overcautious. I tell the truth. Though I might hold back a bit. Out of professional courtesy. I do think it's silly for us to try and make the public think we're all best friends and lovey-dovey. The fact is, once a film is over, we all go our separate ways and seldom meet again, except at a party or an awards show.

Q: No, what I find strange is on a TV talk show, when one star is asked what it was like to work with "X," who may be a holy terror, and all the first star will say is, "It was great," or, "He's very talented, a real pro."

A: I call a spade a spade.

Q: Yeah, you're practically unique, like when you were asked about working with Ms. Dunaway. On TV, everyone acts, as you say, lovey-dovey. In print interviews, they might be a little more open. Jack Nicholson, for instance, after *Chinatown*, said she belonged in an institution.

A: And I'm sure he didn't mean *marriage*....But you know, I must admit that it is easier for a woman to call a spade a spade than for a man. If an actor legitimately criticizes an actress, he is still made to feel like a cad. Much of the audience is very old-fashioned about that, and will write in—nasty letters.

Q: Does anyone read fan letters, period?

A: Well...we all have to pretend we do. I at least have *time* to. Naturally, when one is happily going from project to project, there isn't time enough.

Q: What did Edmund Goulding direct you in?

A: You should know he directed *Dark Victory*. It is the performance of mine that I am most pleased with....*The Great Lie* and *The Old Maid*. Warner asked him to direct *Old Acquaintance*, but Eddie had already helmed *Old Maid*, and [Miriam] Hopkins was in it, and rather than put up with her again, I believe he enlisted in the army!

Q: Is it true you once commented about yourself, "I'm larger than life"?

A: …It *sounds* like me.

Q: I'll bet you've had lots of quotes attributed to you that you never said.

A: [*nods*] But it could be worse. They attribute egotistical things to me. But almost every off-color remark ever said has been attributed to Mae West. She chose sex as her field of expertise, and she paid the price. Of course it is possible she did not mind. *I* have chosen to be an authority on Bette Davis, and that's enough for me.

Q: You said "an" authority. Not *the* authority?

A: No, because for the most part I live in the present. I have to! There is a small army of film experts who are more knowledgeable about my career than I am. They really know it *all*!

Q: At the start of *All About Eve*, when you first appear, the narrator says of Margo, and I quote [*from a piece of paper*], "She is a great star. She never was or will ever be anything less or anything else." He could have been talking about you.

A: [*beams*] People love to draw parallels. But I am not like Margo, really, for she was quite self-destructive.

Q: Is she more closely based on Tallulah?

A: Apparently. Or Elisabeth Bergner.

Q: Rumor has it the relationship of Margo and Eve, which has lesbian undertones [*she winces*], was based on that of Bankhead and her understudy in *The Skin of Our Teeth*, Lizabeth Scott.…

A: Aha…Could be. [*smiles ruefully*] I must say, *I* did not see any of these undertones of which the critics write so often now, until I had seen the film several times. Perhaps I'm just naive. Although I do think it is Eve who is entirely the ambiguous character, not Margo. Stars attract whomever they attract, and not knowingly....Those undercurrents do show up pretty clearly in the final scene, with Eve and her younger [*female*] admirer.

Q: Claudette Colbert was first choice for Margo, if you don't mind my saying so....

A: Mind? Of course not. It's a fact. I had the best piece of luck in my career when she broke her back. Or hurt it. It meant she had to give up playing Margo, and *I* got it!

Q: I cannot possibly imagine Colbert in the role.

A: That's because I've made it my own.

Q: How did you feel when Lauren Bacall played Margo in the musical stage version, *Applause*?

A: At least they did not *film* it. At first I was not pleased. On the other hand, a musical has *nothing* to do with a motion picture. Miss Bacall did a creditable job.

Q: Many people were surprised you got along well with Anne Baxter [*Eve*].

A: Yes. Good actress. No rivalry there, and her part in *Eve* was bigger than mine. But I got the most out of it. My career was revived. I don't think Anne ever got another role as good.

Q: It was her career high point. What about you?

A: Oh, no! High points are always yet to come.

Q: You must have believed you were going to win the Oscar [*a third one*] for *Eve*? [*nods*] However, Gloria Swanson was up for *Sunset Boulevard* the same year, sort of a clash of the titans—Margo Channing versus Norma Desmond.

A: [*emotionlessly*] We canceled each other out. And Fox was behind Anne [*also nominated*], because she was under contract. [*Thus, newcomer Judy Holliday won, for* Born Yesterday.]

Q: Does it hurt that so far you haven't gotten a third Oscar?

A: I did think I would be the first to get three…I was so sure I would get it for *Jane*, partly to make up for *Eve*, but also for my body of work since the first two. Then that Crawford bitch sabotaged me, and when Anne Bancroft won [*for* The Miracle Worker], Crawford got on stage to accept Bancroft's award for her! She'd arranged and schemed, planned everything. She ran a bad-mouth campaign against me.

Q: It must have hurt her that you were nominated but she wasn't.

A: [*fiercely*] Are you excusing her? Of *course* she didn't get nominated…Blanche could have been played by any older actress—no pain, no gain.

Q: Jane Hudson is far and away the more demanding role.

A: And much riskier. I pulled out all the stops. I had to be ugly, inside and out. Charles Laughton once advised me—he said, "Never not dare to hang yourself."

Q: You sure followed his advice, especially on *Baby Jane*!

A: Thank you. People kept saying I was committing professional suicide. I was in my mid-fifties but I looked a zillion! I *cried*, to see what I looked like.…But I had to listen to my own inner voice. People disapproved of many of my film choices, not just during and after *Jane*. After I did *Beyond the Forest* [*1949*], Hedda Hopper wrote that I could not have done more destruction to my career had I planned it!

Q: Looking at *Beyond the Forest* today, one wonders what all the fuss was about?

A: It was *terribly* controversial then! Rosa was a complete bitch. There was an extramarital affair, an unsuspecting husband, the abortion sequence—which was cut in most places. In that era, a man could be dreadful, but the woman always had to have and keep the audience's sympathy—to *some* degree.

Q: You broke that rule more than once.

A: My contribution to ending the double standard...I was hated by many because of it. Women loved me, but many of their husbands loathed me and stayed home! [*laughs*] I didn't play the "little woman." But as I always say, if you please everybody—if that is even possible!—then you *must* be doing *some*thing wrong.

Q: Haven't you stated that it's only when you're controversial that you know you've made it?

A: No, what I said was, anybody can be likable, but it takes guts to be hated. On the screen, that is. For a star to be really a star, half the audience has to love you and the other half has to hate you. They cannot be indifferent to you, or you won't be a star for long.

Q: Like Nastassja Kinski.

A: Who?

Q: Do you think that as a woman and a star, you were so intimidating that you scared off men who might otherwise have made you happy in your private life?

A: [*sighs*] Yes, that is the dilemma. If I'd been a little B-actress, or better yet, not an actress at all, I might have found that one special someone to stay with all my life. But as I wrote in my book *The Lonely Life*, an actress ultimately has to choose between giving up the man or the career. And, really, men do come and go, but as long as one can work, one is fine.

Q: Has it all been worth it?

A: I assume you jest.

Q: Yes. I think it's a dumb question, but one we're supposed to ask.

A: Then I will answer. Yes, it most definitely has been worth it!

Q: Have you often been lonely, as your book's title indicates?

A: ...Lonely in the sense of being without a man in my life. But not *lonely*—being alone is different. In my position, people do not leave you alone! Sometimes I have to tell people I'm going to take time off, for *me*. If I chose to, I could always be surrounded by a crowd, which is *not* the same as having one man with whom to share one's life and hopes and fears.

Q: Which one writer most influenced your career? I know you've given William Wyler the most credit, as a director.

A: Oh, yes, for he made me a true star....My most influential writer would have to be [*W. Somerset*] Maugham. He wrote *Of Human Bondage*, and of course that was my turning point. Star material, at last! Everyone said the movie should have been re-titled *Mildred*, because my role completely overshadowed Leslie Howard's.

Q: If it had been, they'd later have had to re-title *Mildred Pierce*.

BETTE DAVIS SPEAKS   181

A: [*smiles condescendingly*] Yes…something like *Daughter Dearest*. But, getting back to *Bondage*, and with all due deference to Mr. Howard, anyone could have taken his role.

Q: Like Blanche, it was less showy. You know, in the remake, Laurence Harvey was okay, but Kim Novak seemed lost at sea.

A: Remakes are just a pain in the ass! [*shaking head*] Actors only do them for the money, and audiences hate them.

Q: Can we switch to one of the men in your life? Howard Hughes [*with whom Davis had an affair*]…

A: When *I* knew him, he hadn't become so…extreme. My relationship with Mr. Hughes, who was a film producer, is really *too* complicated to go into.

[*Note: Re Davis biographer Charles Higham, Bette claimed she was the only woman who could make the bisexual billionaire reach sexual climax. Bette's second husband, Harmon Nelson, bugged the philandering pair and threatened to send the tape to the press, which would have ruined Davis's career. Hughes then threatened to sue Nelson for invasion of privacy. The affair ended, and Bette paid Howard the damages which he'd demanded from her husband.*]

Q: We'll skip it, then. [*approving smile from the interviewee*] But can we talk some more about Ms. Crawford? It's so seldom that two legendary women work together, plus the feud—or rather, not getting along at all.…

A: [*said with an admonishing finger*] We got along, like the sisters we were playing in front of the camera. Our personal antipathy never interfered with our professional relationship. We had a breakneck pace to keep, and I may say that Miss Crawford was a total pro.

Q: Everyone says she was a pro. Discipline galore, right?

A: [*softens*] Discipline is fine for a set. Too much of it at home is for the birds!

Q: What's eerie is that in the latter part of her career, in *Harriet Craig* and *Queen Bee*, she was virtually playing herself, the character unveiled in the book *Mommie Dearest*.

A: She probably didn't care by then.

Q: Stars hide their unpleasant characteristics on the way up, but tend to revel in them once they're on top. True or false?

A: It depends on *how* unpleasant it is....

Q: Seems to me that after *Mildred Pierce*, Crawford's face— the devouring mouth, the mannish eyebrows—got harder and harder. I can hardly think she did that on purpose.

A: She *drank*...a lot. I understand that tends to change people, women in particular.

Q: What drives a superstar to drink?

A: Private demons. Her childhood, I suppose. Whenever she talked about it in interviews, it was as if it was something recent, and always bitter.

Q: They say most child abusers were themselves abused children.

A: But child abuse is not only physical. It can be the withholding of love. Or compliments. Ruthie was a great believer in compliments, and that was not a popular attitude at the time. People believed spare the rod and spoil the child, but my mother always felt I could conquer any goal, and said so. She helped give me that belief in myself.

Q: As you know, Crawford was famed for her close relationship with the press—answering letters, cooperating with fans and media....She was desperate in her courting of the press.

A: She was smart. It wasn't like today, where the press is ready to tell the worst about everybody. They were a good shield, in the old days. Joan knew that, and now we all know that she had a lot to hide. She did her work well—that's why *Mommie Dearest* raised such an outcry.

Q: Did you feel that you needed the media on your side?

A: Of course. But not to that extent, not to operate out of fear. I had nothing to hide, or nothing much. Certainly nothing more than the average woman. But *I* believed my *work* mattered. Not an image, or maintaining it. I knew if I did my best and worked with the best directors and writers and kept a civil distance from the press, I would be all right. It is the *audience* that makes a star. Not the press, which is even more fickle than an audience.

Q: Is there a Crawford film you really like?

A: She did a number of interesting projects. But she didn't come into her own until...thirty. She was rather the dull ingenue before that. And you know, she did *silents*....

Q: She was, um, before your time?

A: Yes! She began very young. I waited until I had had some training. *Her* training was *not* on the stage [*smirks*].

Q: I don't think she ever did a play.

A: It wouldn't surprise me.

Q: She must have been in a tough spot when she came to Warners from MGM, as you had first crack at the best scripts. You were acknowledged queen of the Warners lot [*Davis was sometimes called "the Fifth Warner Brother"*], but she was also Hollywood royalty.

A: I secretly felt sorry for her. I knew what it must be like for her. Nevertheless, after years of fighting to build myself up at Warners, I was ready and very able to defend my turf.

Q: Did she ever do a movie you wished you'd done?

A: *A Woman's Face*, which her friend Mr. Cukor directed. A complex role—woman with a scarred face and personality. It was a good, literate script....She did a creditable job in *Humoresque*, which wasn't my kind of role—[*John*] Garfield was brilliant in it as the violinist. But then she did all those potboilers, and of course [*sourly*] *she* could get away with it.

Q: What about her wonderful Freudian Western, *Johnny Guitar*?

A: Oh! That was a *scream*! She and that masculine actress [*Mercedes McCambridge*], and their gunfight! It was ridiculous, but entertaining. Rather lightweight, but it does have a following, I'm told.

Q: Crawford declared that long before *Baby Jane*, she'd wanted to team up with you. Professionally....

A: Did she...? Well, in those days, they didn't usually team women.

Q: Yet you worked with de Havilland all those times.

A: But she sometimes played a supporting part.

Q: Which Crawford wouldn't have.

A: She damn well near did in *Jane*! [*triumphantly*]

Q: Her last film was about seven years before she died—

A: Ah! That...monster movie....

Q: No, *Trog* [*1970*], about a prehistoric creature, a troglodyte. My question is, do you think she retired on purpose?

A: [*shakes head firmly*] No. Like me, she would have wanted to keep going till the bitter end. I think she was awfully sad that they only gave her guts-and-gore scripts, and she didn't want to take supporting roles in anything good *or* bad. She was waiting....But you must keep visible, must keep acting. An actor who does not act is not an actor...no. She died bitter and lonely. She hated what her life had become. That will *nevah* happen to *me*.

Q: She even shut friends and relatives out of her life, the last several years. Strange, because she'd been a very gregarious star.

A: But that's *it*: When she was no longer really a star, not a working actress, she didn't want to be among people. Without her work, I don't think she felt worthwhile. Or interesting.

Q: Or very interested.

A: There is *no* need to hole up in an apartment and die alone. No. None. Poor Joan. I *wish* I could have liked her more.

Q: Summing up, what was the biggest difference between Davis and Crawford?

A: [*brightens*] That, I can tell you quickly. I *like* myself. [*pause, for emphasis*] Always liked myself and who I am. If I was a schoolteacher, I would like myself and probably like my life. Even when I wished I was prettier, I liked my personality, my talent. I did *not* go into acting to escape myself, as many, many actors do. I went into it because I found it thrilling.

Perhaps with Joan, her dedication to her public image was an attempt to escape her past or her true self, to *change* herself. I didn't want to change, except on the set. To me, a person is not their looks, but rather what they are inside. When I read biographies, I was most impressed by people who, whatever their looks or background, created something special that they could leave behind to future generations. *That* is what I wanted to do with my acting, not just live a glamorous life and wear pretty clothes. And I certainly nevah tried to keep up with anyone else's standards.

In my work, I could take or leave glamour or beauty. I simply wanted to become someone else as convincingly as I could—for my *work*. But I can assure you that when I go home at night, when I leave the studio, I always know who I am, and it is always *Bette Davis* who departs that studio!

HER DIRECTOR: ROBERT ALDRICH

A two-part phone conversation in mid-1979 with director Robert Aldrich, interrupted by "Sorry, I have to go to the can—I'll call ya back. My age, when ya gotta go, ya gotta go."

A large and bluff man, director-producer Aldrich put his mark upon a staggering variety of films, from Bette Davis's *Whatever Happened to Baby Jane?* and *Hush, Hush, Sweet Charlotte* to the Western *Vera Cruz*, the football flick *The Longest Yard*, the lesbian-themed *The Killing of Sister George*, *All the Marbles*—about female wrestling babes—and *The Legend of Lylah Clare*, about a Garboesque and Sapphic Hollywood legend.

Aldrich had also helmed Joan Crawford in *Autumn Leaves*. The story goes that before Davis agreed to team with Crawford in *Baby Jane*, she asked Aldrich point-blank if he'd slept with—and would therefore favor—Joan. He lied and said No.

BH: What was Joan Crawford really like?

RA: She could switch on and off between fire and ice. Didn't have no middle ground.

BH: And Davis?

RA: She's just as self-involved as the other lady was, but with her, it's more of an adversarial relationship. She has to be very sure of her director before she can relax just a little.

BH: One has heard that *Baby Jane* was a smooth shoot. But it must have been a tense set.

RA: Everyone around them was waiting for the ladies to explode. Never happened.

BH: Both were aggressive survivors, but who do you think was tougher?

RA: Davis is definitely tougher.

BH: In what way?

RA: Hard core. She'll battle till she or the enemy drops.

BH: Did Crawford, by contrast, have more of a desire to appear the gracious lady?

RA: All her Hollywood training, in diction and deportment and all that, was to make her a lady. She could be real grand. She was an elegant dame.

BH: But a dame, right?

RA: A dame is a dame. A lady's a lady.

BH: When you approached the studios for financing, did they really say they wouldn't give you a dime for "those two old broads"?

RA: [*chuckles*] That's what they said. Then Davis got ahold of it and informed the press, and Crawford got miffed. She thought Davis had called her a broad.

BH: But she was only quoting the studio men. So Davis could laugh at herself.

RA: To a degree. That's where she parted company with Crawford, who took herself very seriously.

BH: Were you surprised when Bette was Oscar-nominated and Joan wasn't?

RA: Davis was a standout, but in my opinion she wouldn't have pulled the nomination if the movie hadn't been a blockbuster for its genre. The publicity it generated was boffo, and we all made calculations how much more it might earn if Davis copped herself another Oscar.

BH: You weren't surprised Crawford wasn't up for one?

RA: Nah. She got her one Oscar [*for* Mildred Pierce], and one was all she could ever have hoped for.

BH: Bette maintains that Joan campaigned against her and lost her the Oscar....

RA: Could be. That wouldn't be beneath her. Joan had a lot of spite in her. She could be two-faced and mighty mean when she wanted to.

BH: She seems almost frightening. What led you to having an affair with her?

RA: [*pause*] Seemed like a good idea at the time.

BH: Do directors sleep with their female stars, the better to control them on the set?

RA: That's the biggest dividend of it.

BH: So are you saying that Crawford was prepared to hurt the film's prestige or box office in order to deny Davis the satisfaction of a third Academy Award?

RA: That's the way it looks. Look, once we wrapped [Baby

Jane], I was headed for my next flick, and thinking about the one after that. I left the ladies to their own devices.

BH: *Baby Jane* was advertised with the catch line, "Sister, sister, oh so fair, Why is there blood all over your hair?"

RA: That was not my contribution. The ad campaign indicated a lotta blood that wasn't there. They wanted to bring in younger audiences, knowing that once the older audiences got wind of the subject matter, most of them would stay away.

BH: Davis and Crawford fans preferred to cherish their memories of the stars in their thirties and forties versions?

RA: Older fans didn't like the movie.

BH: The next one you did with Bette was more macabre, with the severed hand and the blood on the ball gown.

RA: The credo in Hollywood is: If A works, give 'em triple-A, next time out.

BH: Davis complained that *Charlotte* was needlessly bloody and horrifying. Do you agree?

RA: It's not as good as *Whatever Happened to Baby Jane?* but it was a follow-up. Same author, same cast—originally. A follow-up's not a sequel, but it's a try to make big bucks following in the footsteps of an earlier movie. Anyhow, Bette did a good job in *Charlotte*, her salary was jacked up, and the conditions were much better, so what the fuck did she have to complain about?

BH: The conditions must have been much more to her liking, for she got Crawford fired, didn't she?

RA: Hold on. I don't want no lawsuit, so I'm not gonna say Bette got Joan fired. But she was replaced [*by Olivia de Havilland*], and Bette was awful glad.

BH: Didn't Joan claim to be ill, before she left the set?

RA: I don't think it's out of line to say Joan got sick, or made herself sick, from the strain of competing with Davis a second time. Davis was doing better, careerwise, than Crawford. She'd been up for the damned Oscar, and once more her role was a lot flashier than Crawford's. Crawford was running scared.

BH: Don't you think it was somewhat Crawford's fault, that once again she opted for a role in which she was well-dressed and -coiffed, playing a likable, one-dimensional character?

RA: Joan always wanted to be the heroine, wanted people rooting for her.

BH: Davis, by contrast, doesn't care what audiences think?

RA: I think she knows that people go to the movie house for something unusual. They want to be entertained or scared. Bette doesn't always want to repeat herself. If Joan could've played the Queen Mother, she'd have been content to repeat herself into infinity. Bette Davis needs a challenge, and brother, she'll drive you crazy trying to meet that challenge.

BH: As an artist, she always meets that challenge.

RA: She usually does, but at no little cost to her cast and crew!

BH: Would you have worked with Davis again?

RA: Not without getting a lobotomy first.

BH: Finally, why do you think *Baby Jane* has become maybe the number one cult movie ever?

RA: Jeez…I figure because it's the greatest S&M movie ever made. Davis is the greatest sadist the movies ever had, and Crawford's no slouch at dishing it out herself. But when they got together for the screen, somebody had to be lowman, and you just knew it wasn't going to be Bette. No fucking way.

NAME-DROPPING

Q: A few names from the silver screen. Could you respond with one or a few words—the first ones that come to mind?

A: Uh-oh. I'll try, Boze. I'll *try*.

Q: Joan Crawford.

A: ...Hollywood's first case of syphilis! [*cackles*] Now, you *mustn't* print that.

Q: Even though she's deceased?

A: People would think I hated her.

Q: But they do, Miss Davis. They do think you hate her!

A: [*amused*] Well....Let's go on with your list.

Q: Remember, these can be one word—pithy or otherwise....Loretta Young.

A: ...Sanctimonious.

Q: Ginger Rogers.

A: The same. But I like her company, even so.

Q: What do you think of her wearing the same youngish hairdo lo these many moons?

A: Well, long hair is for the young or the ethnic. Period.

Q: You had a long wig in *Beyond the Forest*. And it came across as ethnic.

A: Yes, they thought Rosa Moline was very passionate. And somewhat demented. So they made her look Latin. Somebody at Warners suggested going back to the look I had as [*Empress*] Carlota in *Juarez*, where I go mad. Of course, I said no. But we still chose black, raven hair for Rosa.

Q: Speaking of *Juarez*, an expensive costume drama, I read how Warners devised numerous publicity stunts when it was released. The most amazing, because it actually paid off, was when they had a publicist posing as a moviegoer and he told a cabdriver, "Take me to *Juarez*!" and they drove from the East Coast to Juarez, Mexico, and the resultant headlines read, "Fan Drives 2,500 Miles to See *Juarez*!"

A: [*rocks with mirth*] *Nothing* was beneath them! It was wonderful. Good fun, and lots of imagination. No need for vulgarity or sensationalism then [*shakes head*].

Q: You weren't top-billed in *Juarez*.

A: No, of course not. That was Paul Muni, who played Juarez. He even had it in his contract that when he played a historical character, the name of the picture would be the character's name. He was what they called a prestige actor.

Q: Otherwise, Warners would have changed the movie's title, right?

A: They were worried that no one would know who Juarez was. I believe they identified him as "the Mexican Abraham Lincoln."

Q: Funny, because in Mexico, Lincoln is often called "the American Benito Juarez."

A: [*laughs*] Why not?

Q: The list: Errol Flynn.

A: Unprintable!

Q: Ronald Reagan.

A: ...Not much presence.

Q: Garbo.

A: Beautiful!

Q: Talented too?

A: Of course. At what she did. You could easily believe she might die for love or from love. Not *me*—nevah.

Q: Dietrich.

A: Glamorous. Of course, she too was stunningly beautiful. But she was more like a picture—a photograph—than Garbo. Garbo...*breathed.*

Q: More three-dimensional?

A: That's it.

Q: Jean Harlow.

A: I may disappoint her fans by saying so, but I found her more interesting in person than on the screen.

Q: Do you think without the platinum hair she'd have been as big?

A: [*shakes head*]

Q: Clark Gable.

A: We never worked together. He was afraid of me. A very insecure man.

Q: A chauvinist?

A: Of course! That's not what I meant....When he was the biggest masculine star in Hollywood, he still feared poverty, and always carried a bankroll in his pants pocket.

Q: And speaking of the "biggest," even his wife Carole Lombard said he was, uh....

A: Don't be shy [*teasing*]. I read that recently. She was supposed to have said that with one inch less, Gable would have been the queen of Hollywood, not the king. [*rolls her eyes*]

Q: I wonder who the real king was....

A: Chaplin was reputed to be a contender. So was Bogart.

Q: So's one of your friends....

A: [*sits up and leans forward*] Who?

Q: Roddy McDowall.

A: [*laughs with relief*] Oh! [*pause*] Really?

Q: Mae West.

A: That's a hell of a segue!

Q: It is, yet there were longstanding rumors that West was really a man in disguise.

A: Nonsense! I met her, and I *know.*

Q: You *know?*

A: No use asking. I won't supply any details.

Q: Okay, we'll start afresh. Mae West.

A: Well, I loved her because she made me laugh. She was wonderful, so funny and so unique. I never found her sexy or nasty, just amusing. Very self-mocking.

Q: Then what were the censors so indignant about?

A: She was like a man in her relationships—she chose them,

she launched the affairs and she ended them. This was revolutionary, then. Besides, she made it quite clear that a woman could enjoy sex as much as a man.

Q: That must have gotten some insecure censors going....

A: That is why they clamped down. They didn't want other women emulating her.

Q: You met Mae West. What did you think of her?

A: I had always wanted to meet two people in Hollywood. Two not very accessible actresses—Garbo and Miss West. Everyone else, I had either met or didn't particularly care about meeting....Miss West was tiny. Like me, but more like a little old china doll. I think she was a bit scared of me [*smiles*].

Q: With her ego?

A: That's a front, my dear. She always talked that way—the Mae West character. I *became* a character, on the set. She always *was* her character, in public. God knows what she really was like. She didn't let it show.

Q: Humphrey Bogart.

A: I liked him. Down to earth. But I still can't help thinking of him in supporting roles, because he was, in some of my pictures. *Dark Victory*, of course—and so was Little Ronnie Reagan, as I called him.

Q: Is it true that in Hollywood, Reagan's last name was pronounced Ree-gun?

A: Yes, that's what most people said. I don't know just why he changed it to Ray-gun....

Q: At the time, did you have an inkling that either Bogart or Reagan would become a star?

A: A what?

Q: An *inkling*. [*no reaction*] You know, like when there's something special in the air.

A: Like hay fever? [*laughs*] Well, Reagan *didn't* become a star.

Q: Yet he did star in various films....

A: B-movies. Hopalong Cassidy also starred in films, for that matter. Bogart, of course, became a real star...although more so in death than in life, and I prefer it while I can still know it and enjoy it.

Q: I don't know what prompted this quote, but Bogart once said about Joan Crawford that he disliked the lady but she was a true star....

A: Bogey had good taste.

Q: In women?

A: He married Betty Bacall, didn't he? Most actors' taste is in their mouth!

Q: Edward G. Robinson, for instance? The public thought of him as a violent tough guy, but I know he was a kind and very tasteful man, and an art connoisseur. My family knew him.

A: He was Jewish, wasn't he? [*Robinson was born Emmanuel Goldenberg*] Yes, a nice man. He knew art. Wonderful collection of paintings. Now, someone like Errol Flynn, his idea of art would be the pictures of fruit in a slot machine.

Q: Oh, dear. Well, back to the list. Tallulah Bankhead.

A: *She* had good taste in women too—she claimed to have *known* her favorite movie star, who was Garbo. She called her Miss Greta, because she felt "Garbo" sounded too like a man.

Q: Do you know the anecdote about Tallulah and Noel Coward? He was once telling her—her or Beatrice Lillie; this story's been attributed to both—about a new male comic whom the press described as "a male Tallulah Bankhead." And Tallulah snapped, "Don't be redundant, dahling!"

A: [*laughs*] She *was* a character....Which was a problem for her as an actress, because like Miss West, she nevah really stopped being herself—her *own* character. So you could not have either actress playing somebody very different from her own self. Really, what they were was personalities.

Q: Bankhead was a legendary stage actress. Why couldn't she make the transition to film?

A: Too mannered, for one thing. Not quite beautiful enough—she once wanted to trim a millimeter or two off the end of her nose, said it had kept her from being photogenic. Also, I heard she offended Mr. [*Samuel*] Goldwyn. She was at a party, and she sang "Bye Bye, Blackbird." But she sang it "Bye Bye, Jew-bird."

Q: She wasn't anti-Semitic?

A: I think she loved to shock people. She once had Eleanor Roosevelt to her home, and used the toilet while carrying on a conversation with her.

Q: ...Flushed with embarrassment...Anna May Wong.

A: Anna May who?

Q: Not Woo. Wong.

A: That's a strange transition. I know, of course, who Miss Wong was, but—

Q: Not so strange. She and Ms. Bankhead had much in common....

A: *Oh*...as in that Greek island [*Lesbos*]. Well, you know, when someone first mentioned that many, many years ago, I almost quarreled with him. I didn't believe Chinese could be lesbians. Can you imagine? I was so naive. But then, I was a *virgin* when I married, so there you are! [*laughs*] It never occurred to me about Miss Wong, because the Chinese people's traditions go back so far.

Q: So did the ancient Greeks.'

A: Was she a star at all?

Q: She starred in B-films and played servants in A-films—to actresses like Dietrich, Lana Turner, etc. She wasn't allowed, even as a star, to kiss her leading man, because he was Caucasian.

A: Is that right?

Q: It's in the record books—only leading lady forbidden to kiss her leading man.

A: But in her case, it must not have presented a hardship....

Q: Rex Reed [*she groans*] said you were offered the title lesbian role in the screen version of *The Killing of Sister George* [*eventually played by stage star Beryl Reid*].

A: Whatever Mr. Reed may have inferred, the *reason* I was offered first choice was because Mr. Aldrich [*Baby Jane*] directed it. *I* suggested that he offer it to Miss Crawford, instead. It wasn't suited to me, but would have been much more appropriate for her.

Q: Come, now. The role was a butch stereotype.

A: Well...it would have offered her a chance to flex her celluloid muscles [*impishly grinning*].

Q: Can you comment on Joan's bisexuality?

A: What could I say? What *is* there to say?

Q: Since her death, much has been written about it.

A: Hmph! *Since* her death. *After* one's death, they write *every-thing!* [*glowering*]

Q: She was bi, wasn't she?

A: Yes, yes. It was known about her so-called secretaries and live-in lady fans. But…she would *hate* that they are writing all this about her.

Q: I think she'd hate what people might think. Especially if her love life is written up in a negative way. Anyway, the truth comes out eventually, even if the star doesn't.

A: Well, *I* was nevah *there.*

Q: Yet she chased you.…

A: Not literally!

Q: No, of course not. But she did woo you with gifts, and wrote you little notes—

A: That one was always trying to buy friends! [*snappishly*] She was forever sending thank-you cards, and she had fancy stationery with *JC* on it—*Christ!* Gifts…things. She did that to *every*one, even reporters. With that woman, you could nevah be sure what her motives were. [*disgustedly exhales a puff of smoke*] And I sent her presents *back.*

Q: I didn't mean to irritate you too much.…

A: Why stop now?

Q: Sounds familiar. [*she suddenly laughs*] Someone less irritating. Mae West. What did two divas like you talk about in the privacy of her apartment, which I also visited?

A: What did *you* talk about?

Q: Her and her movies, what else? Mostly, she did a well-rehearsed monologue.

A: [*giggles*] Then you know that her home was like a cocoon. Silk-lined, white and gold, overstuffed and comfortable. Rather like a time capsule, from another era.

Q: Did you talk about men?

A: ...She asked me if I had a lover. I said no. She said perhaps I ought to get one.

Q: Did you consider taking her advice?

A: [*startled, then roars with brief, staccato laughter*] No! [*pause*] Apart from a few very personal things that I can't tell you, we talked about beauty secrets. She had wonderful skin. I also wanted to know about her shoes. They had platforms, and I wanted to know how many inches....I wondered about but didn't ask about her legs. I had always been curious, because she always wore long skirts.

Q: They said she had a multitude of shins.

A: [*laughs*] Did she? I don't know how her legs were, but she said the platforms were about a foot tall. She showed us, and they were!

Q: Did you talk about husbands?

A: Well, she didn't ask me about mine, but she mentioned in passing that she had been married once, though they didn't live together as husband and wife.

Q: She hid the marriage, after she became famous. What did she say about the guy?

A: That he was a pillar of cotton to her....One of those who, the moment the wife is famous, comes out of the woodwork and sues her to get some money. *Al*-imony! The world would be a better place without it; it would make more women, and men, have to stand on their own two feet....He obviously was not much of a husband or a comfort to her.

Q: Sounds like the contrary. A pillar of cotton, eh? Did you ever wish you were taller?

A: That is a mark of misplaced ego. I am not egotistical about my looks, certainly not about my *height*. In my time, shorter women were prized. Ingrid Bergman told me that she'd hated being tall. It took her years to accept it. It is difficult, for a tall woman—especially in love scenes, with the man standing on a box or telephone directories.

Q: It can be tough on a man too. Rock Hudson told me he'd felt like a "giraffe."

A: Oh, but he was divine-looking! Personally, not my type, though. I like them a *little* bit ugly. But he was very attractive, in that Greek statue sort of way.

Q: Do you believe in love at first sight?

A: No! *Lust* at first sight, of *course*. I experienced it many times. But love at first sight is a concept that I suspect you writers dreamed up.

Q: One of us...Back to the list. John Wayne.

A: Now, *he* was a good example of the image taking over. Image on one side, reality on another side.

Q: How so?

A: [*shrugs*] Big things: the war hero who did not fight in the war [*World War II*]. This was a big joke in Hollywood, when after the war and during every war thereafter, he proclaimed himself such a champion of war! Of course, our politics clashed....But also the little things: he wore lifts. In his cowboy's boots, but also in his shoes. All Hollywood knew it.

Q: Might that account for his somewhat tottering walk?

A: I don't know. But I nevah forgot how he avoided the war, unlike most of our brave actors. Wayne took an exemption because he was a father of three, I believe. Others had two, three or four children, but they fought anyway.

Q: Another actor who didn't fight was Ronald Reagan.

A: [*throws up hands*] Yes. But let us not pursue Mr. Reagan. People will think we are picking on him! [*laughs*]

Q: Do you think Wayne and Reagan took such an aggressive, even vicious, part in the fifties witch-hunts to make up for not being in WW II?

A: You mean, a phony kind of patriotism? I don't know. *Next* name.

Q: Barbara Stanwyck.

A: [*no response*]

Q: Are you friends at all?

A: No.

Q: May I repeat something I've heard? That when you were ruling Warners' feminine roost, Stanwyck went there [*in 1941*] to star in *Meet John Doe* with Gary Cooper. And that things have been chilly with you two, ever since. True?

A: ...Partly true. *Next* name.

Q: How did Roz Russell become so closely associated with "lady executive" roles when I would have thought you'd be perfect casting for such roles?

A: [*a bit frosty*] I have, of course, played strong women, women who *did* things. But I did not portray a lady president of the USA, unlike Russell or Crawford [*actually, it was Polly Bergen, in* Kisses for My President], and I was never associated with shoulder pads or...those pinstripe men's suits. Or *pants*—that was Dietrich or Hepburn. Miss

Russell had an entirely different career. *I* was never in a *rut*, and I can assure you, if I had played the lady head of a business firm, it would have happened *once*.

Q: Shirley Temple, then.

A: She was adorable! Such a shame she grew up. And out.

Q: But they all do.

A: *Up.* Not necessarily *out.*

Q: In her memoirs, she wrote that a top movie executive once exposed himself to her as a child. Can you believe that?

A: Oh, easily! Half the men running the studios were exhibitionists. Those who had it, flaunted it.

Q: Joan Crawford wrote that Darryl Zanuck showed her a solid-gold cast of his erect phallus, and that it was a whopper. Did anything like that ever happen to you?

A: [*laughs*] Alas, no. Unlike Miss Crawford, I did not inspire men to "flash" in front of me. For better or worse!

Q: Were you ever chased around the casting couch?

A: They wouldn't have dared! [*laughs*]

Q: You must have heard the rumors that Crawford had done some porno films?

A: [*sighs*] Oh, yes. But then, I am one of the few about whom they have never spread such a rumor. It really doesn't signify. They even say it about men, nowadays.

Q: And it's even true, about Stallone.

A: Well, I have nevah seen any of his pictures.

Q: Did you get around to reading *Mommie Dearest*?

A: ...I do have slightly more important things to do than read books about that woman. We had heard the rumors about how she treated her litter. It came as no surprise.

Q: The surprise is that she somehow got herself an award for Mother of the Year....

A: Don't think *that* wasn't broadcast to every podunk village and town in the country!

Q: Moving on—

A: No. Wait. One thing I am going to say about Crawford and about another actress you asked me about. What Joan did—and there is no doubt she *was* very promiscuous—she did relatively discreetly. She covered her tracks. Like adopting all those children [*due to a botched illegal abortion, Crawford was unable to have children of her own*]. Miss Bankhead, on the other hand, talked her head off about it. She flaunted it. That is why she couldn't really make it in this town. Even in her interviews, she had a very loose tongue, and that was taboo. It shocked the public and, most of all, the studios.

Q: You had those notorious "morality clauses" in your contracts.

A: Even so, all manner of scandals happened, but the studios had enough influence and power to cover them up. This they did if the offending star was repentant. If the behavior would occur again and again, the studio didn't bother.

Q: How did they do these cover-ups?

A: Payoffs. Connections with the police and the...district attorney's office. It was a company town, then. Now, movies are just another industry here and, of course, there is far less corruption.

Q: Do you know the most shocking thing about the morality clause? It's *still* in actors' contracts.

A: That is because Hollywood does not shape the times, it is shaped by the times.

Q: The times of decades past. Anyhow, back to our list. Clara Bow.

A: I would not want to call her a slut, but I don't know what else to say. I'll try and be more complimentary about the next one.

Q: Lana Turner.

A: Now you've made it difficult for me.... [*frowns in concentration*] Her name was really Judy, and her hair was brown—if they hadn't changed both... [*shrugs*]

Q: You worked with Rod La Rocque. Which I've read was his real name!

A: He was a silent star. They made him marry that Hungarian cow [*Vilma Banky*]. After silents, both were finished.

Q: A cow?

A: Not the kind that gives milk....

Q: Digressing a bit, what do you think is the biggest difference between movies and television?

A: Aside from size or pay or prestige? [*sneers*]

Q: Aside from all that.

A: I do not think you can separate television from its inferior size. That is what television *means*. A television set is smaller than the adult viewer's body, so we feel superior to it, and we take it with a grain of salt. Or a whole packet! But at the movies, the screen is many, many times larger than life, and so we look up to it, literally, and it's the same relationship we have to our dreams.

Q: Except that Hollywood designs the dreams.

A: Yes. It is, after all, called the Dream Factory.

Q: Such a repetitive dream, however.

A: [*shrugs*]

Q: Pursuing the list, how about Cary Grant? You never worked with him; I imagine you'd have positively swamped him.

A: I learned a *lot* about him from [*costume designer*] Orry-Kelly. They were roommates and so on before Grant came to Hollywood.

Q: Learned...?

A: Read the books. It's all bound to be in the biographies.

Q: Okay. Ray Milland.

A: A shit! Don't ask me why. And it has nothing to do with romance, etc.

Q: Marilyn Monroe, who played Miss Caswell of the Copacabana School of Dramatic Art in *All About Eve*.

A: A *mess*. Poor thing. Nobody imagined she would become a star. A nervous breakdown—*that* seemed inevitable.

Q: Was she a pro?

A: She tried to be. I give her that. I did *like* her. Of course, I didn't give her much thought. Again, anyone could have played little Miss Dumb Blonde.

Q: But to such good effect?

A: ...You're right. But I didn't really think she belonged in film, and certainly she would have been out of her depth on the stage. But a nice girl.

Q: George Sanders, also from *Eve*, also a suicide.

A: Marvelous voice, terrible man.

Q: Something I've always wondered about. Why do you think the script called his character [*Addison DeWitt, for which Sanders got an Oscar*] a "venomous fishwife"?

A: Lately, I get asked that, yet the person to ask is Mr. [*Joseph L.*] Mankiewicz, the writer and director. He might tell you that Addison was based on a couple of important newspaper columnists like Alexander Woollcott.

Q: Who was gay, hence the stereotypical reference....You appeared in *The Man Who Came to Dinner*, and the title character was based on Woollcott, wasn't it?

A: [*nods*] He was Cole Porter's best friend, his other great claim to fame. [*No. Monty Woolley, who starred in* Dinner, *was Cole's pal.*]

Q: Did you know that Anna May Wong played Gale Sondergaard's role in a TV version of *The Letter*, directed [*like the film*] by William Wyler?

A: That's what I heard, and she was *right*—the proper race for it. But Gale was brilliant in it, and except for Miss Wong, we had no Oriental actors then.

Q: Except, for instance, the ones who played Charlie Chan's sons. Why was Chan himself never played by an Oriental?

A: Because he was a hero, so he had to be played by a [*Caucasian*]. That was Hollywood's rule, not mine.

Q: A real shame. My mom's favorite actress, partly because of the physical resemblance, is Susan Hayward. You know, of course, that she was dubbed "the poor man's Bette Davis"?

A: [*smiles*] I'm sure your mother has good taste, but when we worked together [*in* Where Love Has Gone, *with Davis as Hayward's mother*], she wasn't very nice to me. But we will not go into *that*. I have had to discuss it before.

Q: Peter Lawford once played your lover....

A: In *Dead Ringer*, where I played twins. He played the rich sister's lover.

Q: What was he like?

A: Another mess. By then [*1964*], he'd lost it. A supporting actor, little confidence. I had to bolster him, and did. I liked him. He was *in* with the Kennedys, and that was plenty good enough for me!

Q: I'll bet you're a little nicer to your male co-stars than your female ones?

A: What makes you say that?

Q: Because less competition, and you can mother some of them.

A: The very *young* ones…Peter wasn't that young, but he was a mess, and he needed someone to take charge. But I have mothered young actresses and taken an interest in them. I am not one-sided or prejudicial!

Q: No, you have a good heart. I've heard that.

A: Then write it down! Please. [*smiles*]

Q: Spencer Tracy.

A: A tortured soul. A mean drunk.

Q: Tracy and Hepburn.

A: Friends. I imagine that's all.…

Q: Astaire and Rogers.

A: …Or MacDonald and Eddy? I think nothing could be worse than being part of a duo, or any team, professionally. Being *tied* to somebody like that, in your *work*!

Q: Rumors abound that the partners don't even like each other.

A: No wonder! With a marriage, you can seek divorce. With a duo, the studio is in charge, and if you keep making money for them, you're stuck forever!

Q: Especially in the public's mind. How about Montgomery Clift?

A: Personality-plus.

Q: James Dean.

A: The boy who tried everything.

Q: Uh...Fred MacMurray.

A: Personality-minus.

Q: Merle Oberon.

A: Social climber.

Q: Beautiful, right?

A: ...Yes, if you like a face that looks like it's been dipped in wax.

Q: One of my favorites, Melina Mercouri—who's sometimes described as a Greek Bette Davis....

A: [*clasps both arms of her chair, then slumps back*] Not *really?* She sounds like a man!

Q: Do you think so? She has a great, throaty voice.

A: Augh!

Q: Smoking does deepen a voice over the years, doesn't it? [*she glares warningly*] Like Lucille Ball's...?

A: [*no response*]

Q: Heading for the finish, let me ask you, of the Golden Age stars you didn't work with, who would you most like to have worked with?

A: [*shakes head vigorously*] I do *not* think that way. If it was a really good part, I did not require a big star with me. For a long time—*quite* a long time—I had the pick of the best stories and writers in the world. Best directors. So my only regrets are about stories that didn't get filmed, not people I didn't act with. And those regrets are few, considering.

Q: When Crawford withdrew from *Charlotte*—

A: She was *fired.*

Q: I forgot.

A: Well, I didn't.

Q: You had approval of her replacement, and reportedly vetoed Katharine Hepburn and Vivien Leigh. True?

A: Hepburn and I might have worked together, but not in that sort of picture. Joan was more suited to those roles. And Miss Leigh would have been all wrong for the part of Miriam [*de Havilland*], because Miriam was a Southern belle.

Q: [*I do not contradict Davis by noting that Leigh's two Oscars were for Scarlett O'Hara and Blanche DuBois.*] About *Baby Jane*, the way I heard it was that Crawford found the story, and since she'd been wanting for years to work with you, she—

A: I do not know who found it, but [*producer-director*] Robert Aldrich got it moving, and approached us about starring.

Q: Had you ever wanted to work with Crawford?

A: Not particularly.

Q: You accepted on condition that you play the title role. Could you have conceived of playing Blanche and Crawford playing Jane?

A: Oh, no. Not *her* as Jane. Couldn't have, and wouldn't have. Naturally, I could have played Blanche, the weak sister, but what for? It certainly wouldn't have been a challenge. I *like* a challenge!

Q: Would you say that life is a challenge, or even an uphill battle?

A: Well, it *certainly* ain't downhill! Not for *me*.

HER FRIEND: JOAN BLONDELL

$\mathcal{M}$id-1978. Lunch and an interview at Hollywood's Roosevelt Hotel. The session is for *Hollywood Studio*, a nostalgia magazine to which movie buff Joan Blondell is partial. "I love the past and cherish it," she enthuses, "but I don't live in it." Nor work in it. In 1978, she was seen as a waitress in the John Travolta musical hit *Grease*.

Blondell and Bette Davis had studied together at New York's Anderson-Milton School, and the two worked together in Hollywood in the thirties, remaining friends for over half a century until the former's death in 1979.

BH: I imagine Bette Davis to be a good and loyal friend.

JB: And generous. She's all that, and more. It's not easy to get to be her friend, because unfortunately she doesn't make new friends easily. It's easier if you knew her in the *old* days. Like any star, she has cause to be suspicious. So, friendship with Bette is rare and precious. But she's always there, if you need her.

BH: Is she a demanding friend?

JB: She can be. But she's not as intense about it as she is about her work relationships. For instance, she doesn't call me up at three in the morning, like she's been known to do with directors!

BH: When you worked together in the 1930s, you were both stars. Did your relationship alter in later years, when she was the bigger star?

JB: [*smiles*] I know just what you're driving at. Did she expect me to pay court? No. Because we go back so far. People forget, she sometimes wants to be treated as a friend, not a household name. I never treat her any different, whether she's had a big hit behind her or a long dry spell.

BH: One sometimes hears that she's made life difficult for others, but hasn't her own life been hard?

JB: I'm glad you bring this up. Because she *has* had it hard. Her father left home when divorce was a dirty word, and her ma, Ruthie, had to become man of the house, then Bette took over the responsibilities and had to look after her ma and sister. It's not been easy,—financially or emotionally. In addition, Bette had to fight the industry in a way I never did. I was cute and perky and blonde, in big demand in those days. I still had my figure.

Bette wasn't your typical beauty. She looked different and acted different. She was nervous and ambitious. Guys in the studios didn't know how to peg her. You know how it is with "different"—people don't want ya till you make money for them. Especially an actress, 'cause in those days we either played hookers or molls or girlfriends or wives. Period. The Depression was a real butch, man's-man time.

BH: Was her personal life, as a wife, also difficult?

JB: That's what she probably likes least to talk about. Her husbands, up till Merrill, didn't amount to much. By today's standards, forget it—they were quick to raise their voices and their fists, which wasn't so remarkable. Bette's a lot more sensitive than she lets on.

BH: She impresses as being almost invulnerable.

JB: She's toughened herself—had to. The tragedy of Margot would crush most mothers. And Bette's always the first to attack. She's lost a lot of her early sensitivity, but she deals with people by putting them on the defensive.

She's also had more than her share of physical ailments and accidents. Do you know she broke her back once in a freak accident? It could only happen to Bette. She was inspecting a house, opened a door she thought was a closet, marched through, and plunged down the steep cellar steps onto a concrete floor. Twenty feet! But this is also Bette: Six months later, she was in New York, doing a TV show! Nothing stops her.

BH: Her strength is sometimes criticized, but it seems to me she couldn't have made it without it.

JB: Her biggest secret should be obvious to anyone who's spent time with her, as you have. Bette has boundless energy—it takes plenty of energy to be a star. Not just to become one, to *stay* one. And Bette has it. Nothing keeps her down. She's the next thing to hyper.

She's that way about everything. She cannot relax. Not for long. Loves beautiful scenery, but gets bored looking at it. She was on the go at the studio, days; and nights she must have been restless at home, with her husbands.

BH: What does she do to try to relax?

JB: She doesn't even try anymore. Some of us, her friends, tried to get her to take up a hobby or sport. Unh-unh. She doesn't play games. Part of it's because when she does something, she wants to be good at it. She doesn't want friends to see her doing a sport badly, while next to her somebody's showing off what a great golfer or tennis player he is.

BH: Always competitive?

JB: Always thinking about her work. On vacations, she misses her work! Not me, honey. Give me life nice and slow...Bette also worries about things I couldn't even dream up, like riding a bike. When she was very young, she avoided learning how—she thought if she injured herself, she wouldn't be able to act!

BH: Do you think she makes life unnecessarily difficult for herself?

JB: I can't put myself in her shoes, because we have diametrically opposed personalities. Which is probably why we're still friends! I'm not going to say she should have given up more for her marriages. Who's to say which partner should do more giving up? But Bette isn't a talent when it comes to compromise. Not with a man, especially. With her lady friends, she can be a doll, and take the backseat now and then.

But there's something about a man who might put one over on her....She loves men, but she doesn't trust them.

BH: Would that go back to her father's desertion of his family when they needed him most?

JB: It goes back to that, but I think she's also never forgotten or forgiven the way she was greeted in Hollywood. Or wasn't greeted. Like the boss's son at Universal saying she had less sex appeal than Slim Summerville, or the nicknames—like "sexless little brown wren"—or the cracks about her bug-eyes, and so on. She had to struggle every inch of the way for her recognition and her stardom. Then once she got it, she never believed they wouldn't try and take it away from her.

GOLDEN *Y*EARS

Q: Here in your apartment you have a pillow reading "OLD AGE ISN'T FOR SISSIES." What does it mean?

A: It means if you want to make it into and through old age you have got to stop whining. Complaining, especially nowadays, is the province of the young. They don't realize how good they have it! In my day, if a teenager or young person had carried on like this, they'd have been told to shut up! Or they'd have been slapped.

Q: Or "boxed on the ear"?

A: Yes! Nowadays, you can't do that. If one tries to discipline a young person, they're likely to shoot you in retaliation [*throws up her hands in despair*].

Q: Looking back at your personal life, as opposed to your brilliant career, what do you most regret?

A: …I suppose the end of my last marriage. When it ended, I knew it was goodbye to marriage. I'd have been insane to try a fifth time. When my fourth husband no longer was my husband, it hit me—it devastated me to think—that I would never again be the most important person in somebody else's life.

Q: It's a sobering thought.

A: It may be, but it's the sort of sentiment that could drive one to drink!

Q: Did you have romances since your final marriage?

A: I'm glad you chose "romances" and not "affairs." *That* would be rude. [*taps cigarette ash into ashtray*] I have to admit that even now I still get crushes. But I'm at a point where I think it's better and wiser to admire someone from afar.

Q: Like the knights of old, in unrequited love?

A: Well, unrequited may be scoffed at today. Today, everyone wants instant gratification. But unrequited is probably the smartest thing. It never disappoints.

Q: Would it be too personal to ask which of your husbands you loved best?

A: No, but I'm a Yankee optimist. Each time I fell in love again, it was for the first time.

Q: On the screen, you've portrayed and displayed so many emotions that—

A: It's—what you're saying—rather like that line, in a poem somewhere, about the old woman who indulges and dramatizes all her emotions, just to prove she still has them. But enough about that.

Q: You're so nice and slim, do you exercise?

A: *Hate* exercise! Jumping, bending over...all that. Exercise is for people who get paid to do it!

Q: Do you eat a lot?

A: Do I look like it? [*laughs*]

Q: You've been described—see if you agree—as "the most starry of actresses and the most actressy of stars."

A: [*tilts head pensively to one side*] Interesting...at least whoever wrote that used both terms. I used often to take exception to being called a star. And then, of course, they started calling people superstars, and calling everyone over forty a legend! Now, I don't object, because, really, if anyone is a star, I am. [*quickly adding*]

   Though naturally I continue to think of myself as an actress, foremost.

Q: Your trademark speech pattern was criticized almost from the beginning—your biting of your consonants, etc.

A: Oh, my, yes! [*sighs*] It does *not* faze me. At one point or another, everything about me has been criticized....This is to be expected. I cannot complain too much, because I long ago realized that criticism implies that people care....

Q: True. If they don't give a hoot, your name probably won't even show up in print. If you were starting out today, do you think that with today's macho-oriented and juvenile-oriented market, you'd still become a star?

A: Probably not. Again, I was extremely lucky in my times and timing. *But*. [*long drag on cigarette*] Your question presumes that I would choose to be an actress, and back in the 1920s, women had very few options. A nurse or a teacher or an actress—very few other choices. If I were young today (and heaven forbid!) I might choose to become a doctor. They certainly are more needed than ever now.

Or I might have chosen law or politics. We need good politicians more than ever! There is so *much* to choose from.

Q: Can you think of anything, offhand, that you wouldn't choose?

A: An acting coach! [*shakes head pityingly*] They say most of them are frustrated actors, but if that is so, then they should be out seeking work. No actor is too old to work, if the desire is there.

Q: Can acting be taught?

A: No, it can only be improved on, and *that* is done by acting, not by sitting in a class listening, and not by telling young people how it is supposedly done!

Q: Does the prospect of leaving your apartment unaccompanied disturb you?

A: Ten or twenty years ago, it wouldn't have. Of course, I would have been ten or twenty years younger....But now, young men are no respecters of age, and small children and elderly people are victimized for their very defenselessness.

Q: Do people ever bother you when they recognize you?

A: I am happy to say that everyone still recognizes me....All in all, my privacy is respected. I am not antisocial, but there is a time and a place. And an attitude. Not long ago, I was in a restaurant. A young man came up and requested my autograph—no enthusiasm or deference in his voice, no excitement in his eyes. As for older fans, they will recognize me, but often they just look—it may be they are intimidated!

Q: You must be an authority on how people look when they're awestruck.

A: [*inclines head graciously*] You see, that young man clearly had no interest in me. What he was even doing in this type of fine restaurant, poorly dressed and ill-kempt, I don't know. I imagine somebody told him an autograph from Bette Davis might be valuable someday....

Q: After so many years, is signing autographs a bore?

A: Boze, when they stop asking for your autograph, that's when you know your pan is losing its shine!

Q: Angela Lansbury said she asked you for your autograph. Is a request from a peer or colleague more exciting than one from a typical fan?

A: They are all very flattering [*looking at ceiling*].

Q: Please tell me if this story is true. You were in the lobby of a Madrid hotel, and Ava Gardner came up to you somewhat shyly and said something like, "Oh, Miss Davis, I've admired you for so many years." And you replied, "But of course you have, my dear," and swept majestically out.

A: [*laughs*] The question is, do *you* believe it?

Q: I think I'd like to. It's so Bette Davis.

A: [*smiles, shakes head*] I can't remember....

Q: You can't remember if you were in Madrid or you can't remember if you met Ava Gardner?

A: Of course I can remember being in Madrid! Just don't ask me the year....

Q: But you don't remember being in Madrid and meeting Ava Gardner?

A: [*an exasperated sigh*] Well, one meets so many people....

Q: Who of today's actresses, if any, do you admire?

A: A popular question [*sourly*]. But I *too* am one of today's actresses.

Q: I know. But, um, in the seventies you said you admired Glenda Jackson above her contemporaries.

A: Yes, she is excellent. Like me, she got to play Elizabeth I twice—for television and the screen.

Q: They asked that question of Joan Crawford, and her response was Faye Dunaway.

A: Ye gods! Well...,that figures.

Q: Of the eighties bunch, who do you like?

A: [*resigns herself*]...Streep is good, of course, and in the Academy's good graces, but can she carry a movie? I had to be good *and* turn a profit, else no matter how good I was or how many awards I won, I'd have been demoted to support or put out to pasture. I had films built around me. This does not happen today.

Q: Streisand and Fonda?

A: They're the last....

Q: She-stars: an endangered species?

A: Don't laugh, it's true.

Q: Women used to be at least half of the box-office champs. What changed all that?

A: Television. [*pause*] Older people stopped going to see what they could get at home for free.

Q: But most moviegoers are young. Do they only like male stars?

A: It has to do with marriage, and it's very simple: when a boy and girl are courting—or "dating"—*she* lets *him* pick the film. To give him an illusion of control. And men always prefer watching heroic versions of themselves on the screen. In the old days, men preferred to watch Cagney and Gable and Bogart. Women came to see *my* movies, or those of Garbo, Stanwyck, etc.

But once a couple is married, they stay home, and the wife chooses what they watch on TV.

Q: Which is why there are various series starring women?

A: Exactly.

Q: Thank you for explaining it all to me [*she actually nods*]. Can you think of a male star from your heyday who wouldn't be a star in today's action-oriented Hollywood?

A: Oh, easily! Herbert Marshall [*most memorable as Bette's tormented husband in* The Letter *and* The Little Foxes]. Because of his wooden leg. In those days, it would have been thought terribly rude even to mention he had a wooden leg [*due to World War I*]. It was never printed. Now, of course, there are no taboo subjects, so Mr. Marshall would be out. Which is unfortunate. It's also why someone like Franklin Roosevelt could never become president today. Because of his handicap. He wouldn't even get nominated to run, now that the package is everything.

Q: And the substance counts for so little.

A: Here's something true for you: Herbert was visiting the home of some non-actor friends of his, and after lunch he tripped over something in their living room. He fell to the floor, and the hostess mistook his embarrassment for pain. She didn't know what to do. So she turned to her husband and asked, "Should we call a doctor? Or a carpenter?"

Q: That's cute—I think. Your last stage fling was [*she groans*] the aborted stage vehicle *Miss Moffat*, an updating of *The Corn Is Green*. You clashed with [*the late director*] Joshua Logan, and it was a fiasco. Why?

A: Well, everyone in the business knows he's a manic-depressive. He was impossible to get along with! A bully.

Q: No room for bullies on the set, right?

A: *One* [*points to herself, smiling*]. A terribly bitter disappointment it was, too. Even though I was finally the right age to play her.

Q: Logan told the press your moods tired him out.

A: Hah! [*angrily, succinctly*] I may be manic about my work, but I do *not* give in to so-called moods. *He* should talk! He was too old to direct—he was past it. And he was used to bossing women around.

Q: It's said he clashed with Mary Martin on *South Pacific*, then vetoed her for the movie version.

A: He chose another actress for the film because he said Mary Martin had the sex appeal of a cocker spaniel. And they were *friends*.

Q: Ouch. But Mitzi Gaynor was younger than Mary Martin....

A: Age discrimination.

Q: Are you sometimes amazed at the proliferation of star biographies and memoirs?

A: Not really, because we do lead the most colorful lives. But I am flabbergasted at what is sometimes revealed. Having lived through it all and survived, I get frequent requests, usually by mail, to be interviewed about this or that personality. Sadly, the would-be author doesn't want to know what it was like to work together. Or to collect accurate details. He or she wants only the "dirt."

Q: So you turn them down?

A: Most of the time, yes. Of course. Because all they want from me is an anecdote or a quotable quote, preferably something bitchy or rude. Well, I was brought up in a time when one spoke about oneself, not others. It isn't polite to ask me about someone else and never inquire about *me*. If a writer interviews me about *my* life and career, then they can learn something about X or Y along the way. But to ask me to just talk about Y…Hmph!

Q: Why don't they ask Y?

A: Well, in my case, X, Y and Z are usually dead! [*laughs*]

Q: What's it like being the lone oak in the forest?

A: …It's rather threatening, in a way, because as everyone from my time at Warners dies off, it seems as if a lot of my past is going with them. No one left who remembers, no one to remember it with—not that one picks up the phone and rehashes old times. Most of these people, I haven't seen in years—twelve or twenty or more years. But knowing they're no longer *there*.…

Still, mustn't complain. *I'm* here. In the long run, it really is a benefit, being a woman. All those golden age stars—the men—people like Gable and Cooper and Errol Flynn and this one and that one, usually dying by age sixty!

Q: The average lifespan of a male actor does seem quite short. While the women often last into their eighties and nineties. I'm sure we could each come up with a quick and lengthy list.

A: The public thinks we all live the life of Riley [*shaking her head*].

Q: Whose life do you live?

A: An artist's life is nevah really easy, young man. For actors, it's worse. Rightly or wrongly, many think the current assignment might be the last.

Q: The difference is, most people can't retire in comfort on the basis of their last few paychecks.

A: You're talking about stars.

Q: Aren't you? I'm willing to bet character actors live longer than the Gables, Coopers and others.

A: They probably do…if they're not too ambitious.

Q: Do you hate it when biographies come out about you?

A: Generally. Because, inevitably, they twist so many facts. But, almost as bad, they omit so many others.

Q: Like?

A: The *nice* things I did! They just want to write about a bitch! They insist on taking my more memorable roles—and the most memorable are usually the bad girls—and pretending *that* was me! It does hurt.

Q: Is it like the news, where they say viewers only want the disasters, not the good deeds?

A: [*loftily*] I don't know how or if my life compares to the news. In this town, when you turn on the evening news, it boils down to who was murdered that particular day....Those biographers only want to dramatize, and yes, my career has been filled to overflowing with drama. But not so much my private life. Nobody rages *all* the time! They exaggerate or invent, and the balance is never there—the nice, ordinary things one does.

Q: Can you be specific, Miss Davis?

A: Of course I can't. One doesn't list one's good deeds. It would be asinine. And it would leave one open to the charge of being, again, egotistical. One doesn't do good deeds to have them repeated, although it wouldn't hurt if they were!

Q: We tend to mold our icons, don't we?

A: Well, I hope *you* don't.

Q: In what I've read about you, there is a pattern of female-bashing. The same aggressive outlook or healthy in-fighting would go pretty much unremarked on, say, Kirk Douglas or Jimmy Cagney.

A: If women wrote more biographies, it would improve things somewhat. The worst are those British tabloid types, those working-class louts who are mad at the world and loathe successful females. They try to crucify you!

Q: Do you refer to someone in particular?

A: I wouldn't waste my breath naming him, if I did!

Q: Only you could get away with some of your quotes, Miss D. Is this a true one? When you toured with de Havilland to promote *Sweet Charlotte*, you reportedly told her, "You were very good, Olivia. When I wasn't on the screen, you still managed to hold the audience's interest."

A: You mean is it true she held the audience's interest? Of course she did.

Q: Is it true you gave her a backhanded compliment?

A: [*laughs merrily*] Olivia is my dear friend, and one of my oldest—in a chronological sense, obviously. She is younger than me, as I freely admit. But let me tell you something, Boze. Some quotes were never meant to be quotes, even when they aren't exaggerated. I think eavesdropping is despicable, and some comments are made in jest or are not meant to be overheard.

Q: That's understood. Tell me, was it difficult leaving New England, where you'd lived for so long, to move back to Hollywood?

A: New England is my home, where my roots are. But the roots aren't as strong anymore, and I had to come here. To be where the work is.

Q: You'll never retire, but don't you imagine women like Garbo or Irene Dunne must regret having retired so long ago, in middle age?

A: I would go *insane*. I am sure those ladies regret it—now and then, at least. Although perhaps not Garbo so much. She was so very beautiful, and it would have been sad to watch that beauty disintegrating before our eyes.

Q: Joan Collins said that when one has mere beauty—though, of course, Garbo had more than that—it's like a rich person becoming a little bit poorer, every single day....

A: Marvelous quote! Very true. I can *now* say that fortunately I never had great beauty.

Q: What physical characteristic on a classic beauty did you most envy?

A: [*recoiling slightly at "envy"*] Cheekbones...Hepburn's, also the way Dietrich's flared out when she smoked. But anyone's good cheekbones, really.

Q: Does it depress you that Hollywood gives so little respect to the older actress?

A: [*snorts*] Hollywood respects money, period. If it hadn't been for *Jane*, I might have done nothing on-screen in the sixties. I might have had to move to England, where it was somewhat better. *Jane* made a lot of money, so they grew interested in me again. Hollywood did not take me back out of affection, I can assure you!

Q: Who *is* Hollywood, today?

A: Bankers.

Q: And in the past?

A: Moviemakers, with the bankers on the sidelines—not in the center of things, which is why today's movies are the pits. The bankers want every product to be a hit. The greed today is beyond belief!

Q: Getting back to biographers, is there anything specific they've misrepresented about you?

A: [*laughs contemptuously*] I resent it when they write that I deliberately tried to dominate my pictures. Or I didn't want the competition of big-name leading men. This all simply happened. If it was a Bette Davis picture, people went. There was far more loyalty to stars then. It didn't have to be a Davis and Gable picture. He had his big following, I had mine. Nowadays, they have to team three or four big stars, and even then, there is no guarantee.

Q: You were sort of a starmaker. Various of the men you worked with, like Bogart or Reagan, became famous after working with you.

A: They probably didn't have much of a chance to shine, with me around! [*giggles*]

Q: What's the worst thing about being older?

A: *Old*, you mean. Thank you [*smiles*]. [*long pause*] I'm trying to think where to start....

Q: Hepburn told someone that when people inquire after her health, she says, "Fine, so long as you don't ask for details."

A: [*laughs*] One of the worst things, which I will *not* detail, is dentures.

Q: Discomfort?

A: And often agony. End of subject.

Q: Are there any advantages to old age?

A: ...Respect is supposed to be one of them, but we've moved away in this country from respecting anything, haven't we? I suppose one advantage of age is it gives you license to act eccentric or be moody and get away with it! Of course, in my case, people always expected me to be a total witch, and now, when I act like a normal person, they're amazed and delighted by my conduct.

Q: Are you a shouter?

A: Are *you*?

Q: Hardly ever.

A: No, not often...Well, that isn't really true. You see, I'm very firm about where I stand. I don't like confusion around me, and I try nevah to confuse people. They do know where I stand, and they can take it from there. Particularly on a set. My name is attached to a project, so that project represents me to the outside world. I have developed a reputation for a certain level of quality, and if people work with me, they must do their very best so that quality there will indeed be!

Q: So you do shout now and then.

A: Of course. When I have to. I had misunderstood your question, because shouting is not the same as making scenes. I nevah make a scene—I don't have to. This is an advantage of age for a star; a young star is deferred to, but an old one—a legend—is in some quarters practically worshipped!

But as I've said, adulation is nice, but it doesn't entirely compensate for working less often than one would like.

Q: You'd said that your past sort of dies away when your colleagues from Warner Bros. die. But all those wonderful motion pictures are left behind, today and tomorrow....

A: Yes, of course. Celluloid is forever.

Q: Closest you can come to immortality.

A: As long as it's not *color*ized! Mediocre immortality doesn't measure up [*shaking head*].

Q: The man you declare made you a true star, William Wyler. Is it true you nearly married him?

A: Absolutely true. It would have been very interesting being married to a director, and a great one. But I did love Willie, regardless of our ups and downs, and he knew it. We didn't marry because of a silly argument.

Q: It wouldn't be because he was Jewish?

A: Heavens, no! Have you *read* that?

Q: No, but there's an author who said recently—and he didn't say what he based it on—that you're anti-Semitic.

A: He is a liar! [*clenching fists*] Willie was Jewish, and that is good enough for me! How *dare* people say such things! Who is he? Is he a friend of yours? Tell him, if you ever meet him again, that he ought not to spread libel, or he could find himself in serious *trouble*! Stupid bastard! He is totally wrong. I would have had no *career*—Warner was Jewish, Wyler was Jewish, practically *every*body connected with my films and work was Jewish, so how could I *possibly* be against them?! I am *grateful*...[*still fuming*].

Q: I thought he had to be wrong.

A: One hundred percent wrong. In *no* way am I bigoted. On the contrary, as has been written about me, I was ahead of my time in promoting blacks and gays and everyone else. Women, of *course*, too. Mr. Wyler was probably the single most important person in my entire career.

Q: You reportedly dislike weak directors.

A: Well, the director is the father of us all, on the set. His primary care has to be for his actors and script. By God, he'd better know where he wants to guide them to, or he's *out*. There are too many egos and too much money on the line for any director to be wishy-washy.

Q: How would you feel working for a woman director?

A: I'd be as hard on her as I would be on a man. An actor *wants* to look up to his director, but the director must walk that fine line between being an incompetent fool and a castrating dictator.

Q: That's some line.

A: Well, the best sort of director is the iron fist in the velvet glove, but he is *very* rare.

Q: Has age made you less ambitious?

A: No. Just more realistic. In the old days, there were so many good scripts thrown my way. I always got first crack, once I'd established myself. It was a question of what to play? I declined *Gone With the Wind*....Now, at my age, but also because of the times we live in, there are almost no good scripts. It is more the difficult question of taking an existing novel or play and getting someone to make a decent screenplay out of it. As I keep wishing they would do with *Ethan Frome*.

Q: Do you still get horror scripts submitted to you?

A: [*rolls eyes, shakes head*] As long as I live, I will get horror scripts. They have gone from horror to horrendous, but it is inevitable. *Jane* was a big hit, and everyone still watches it. It is how so much of the younger public sees me. I wish they would see me in pictures I did before the 1960s, and perhaps thanks to videos, there is a chance....Of course, I turn down these horror scripts, because they don't have one-tenth the quality *Jane* had. If you ever write a script, do *not* let greed be the main reason—or it will *show*.

I find it strange and even sexist that prominent actresses in my age group are the targets of horror films. Old age is indeed rather horrifying, but no less so for old men.

Q: Have you ever wanted to be a man?

A: No, no, no, not at all! "Penis envy" is a stupid thing, *if* it even exists. No. I love being a woman. [*smiles coquettishly*]

I love being alive. At least, I keep telling myself I do [*laughs*]. I do.

Q: Is time really the great leveler?

A: [*sighs*] In many ways. One can be famous and rich, but in old age one still suffers most of the same ills. All the money on earth cannot buy perfect health or freedom from pain. And money....In one's youth, being rich is a wonderful thing, it does make life easier. In old age, it can bog you down a bit. It means you have to have suspicions about how your money is being handled and who wants to get at it. People's motives, and all that. It gets to be a real bore.

Q: Yet you seem to have a sense of humor about aging.

A: Otherwise, it would kill you! Time is so relentless. It brings people into situations they could not have imagined....But I don't want to sound like a pessimist. I'm not, quite. Time is kind, in a way. Because it is so very slow. Old age creeps up on one, ever so slowly, so gently.

Q: "On little cat's paws," somebody said.

A: [*smiles warily*] Sweet. Thank *heaven* age is so slow, because the difference between what we see in the mirror now and what was there ten or twenty years ago is tremendous! Day by day, one only sees imperceptible change. If one looked fifty, then woke up next morning and looked in the mirror and saw oneself seventy, why, it would *kill* you! From the shock and the heartbreak.

Q: There's one of your top directors we've almost ignored—

A: Directors have less ego than we actors. They don't mind not being mentioned, as long as you like their work. With an actor, that would be impossible.

Q: Irving Rapper, who's still alive, directed you in *Now, Voyager*, to name one. And I recently saw you on a 1971 *This Is Your Life*, where you and co-star Paul Henreid actually put down Mr. Rapper. What was the reason?

A: [*with strained patience*] I know he claims that he came up with Paul's lighting of two cigarettes at the same time. But Paul was really responsible for that, and we both created a lot of business in our various scenes. I felt rudderless—Mr. Rapper was not lending a directorial hand.

Q: You worked with him on a number of films....

A: And they turned out well anyway.

Q: Was there a personal antipathy between you?

A: I'd rather not go into that.

Q: Even if it clears the record?

A: [*shakes head*] Unpleasantness leads to more unpleasantness. After that tribute show you mentioned, he went around saying terrible things about me. I *don't* want to give him ammunition.

Q: Like, if he writes an autobiography?

A: Hah! Anyone who thinks you cannot change history has nevah read an autobiography!

Q: By contrast, you got on famously when Henreid directed you in *Dead Ringer*, soon after *Jane*.

A: Well, he knew who was boss.... [*smiles, then breaks out laughing*] I was teasing you! You see how ready you are to believe the legend of Bette Davis? The *director* is the boss on a set. Always. But Paul did give me considerable leeway, for I was playing twins, which is not easy and is technically demanding. I needed a director who could help me, not a traffic cop and not a chauvinistic adversary. I make certain inquiries about my directors *before* agreeing to work with them. Some men look forward to the chance of directing and taming Miss Davis; I nevah give them the chance....

Q: You mean you don't work with them?

A: I do if the script is good enough. I love a fight—if it's worthwhile. I will not argue about trivia. But I either don't work with those directors, or *I* tame *them*.

Q: Which is also part of the Davis legend.

A: A true part [*proudly*].

Q: You know that you've been described in print as the "bitch goddess—"

A: A term of *affection*.

Q: Right. Besides your courage, what really drew you to all those bitchy roles?

A: *That* is the question....I don't deny that something in me was attracted to playing such women. Something basic, but perhaps subconscious. I have asked myself that question, but I've never really found the answer, and I don't think I want to....

Q: Who, then, is Bette Davis?

A: [*beams*] An actress from New England. A *good* actress. One whom people have learned to love.

EPILOGUE: GALE SONDERGAARD

*A*llow me to steal Bette Davis's spotlight for a moment! In this business, we all have various identities, and people know Bette as Margo Channing, as Jane Hudson, as several fiery young characters, and as a hellcat-on-wheels. I myself am the Spider Woman from the films I made as that character. I am also the first actress to win a supporting Academy Award. I am the wife of Herbert Biberman—one of the Hollywood Ten. I was personally blacklisted for two decades—and don't ever let the Ronald Reagans tell you that there was no blacklist! I am also known as the Eurasian woman who made Bette Davis buy *the letter*.

Because our characters in *The Letter* were so vivid, and it was such a success and is an all-time classic, some people assume I worked often with Bette. About a year before, we each participated in another Warner film, *Juarez*. And that's that. Bette and

I were not and are not chums. My primary relationship to her, besides the obvious one of colleague, is an admirer, like those who will read your interviews with her.

Recently, I've been asked if Bette and I were enemies—because of our roles in *The Letter*—or close friends. Neither. I have also been asked if she befriended me during the McCarthy era, or whether she shunned me during that blacklist. The answer is neither. She remained in contact with me, and the truth is, as an individual and as a star, she could have done more to protest something which should never have happened in our country. But, then, that is true of most stars and most people.

But as an actress, she could not have done more. And I choose to end this document on a positive note! Bette is not one of those insecure stars who insist upon always being cast as heroes or role models. For, to court perennial popularity or to never show a flaw on screen is to restrict oneself as an artist. Bette has the guts to be hated by those filmgoers who believe an actor is the character. Like few of her status, she has tried to force reality onto the screen and to grow as a performer. She trusts in the intelligence and discernment of her fans, and brings her full conviction to any role she portrays.

Bette's honesty is reflected in her offscreen persona. If asked a question, she will usually answer it honestly. You don't know how rare this is in Hollywood! I imagine that your interviews with Bette Davis will entertain her legions of fans and offer insight into the unusual and gutsy legend that she has dared to be!

Gale Sondergaard
Hollywood, 1981

INDEX